Spiritual Healing

"...They rely on empty arguments, they utter lies; they conceive trouble and give birth to evil. They hatch the eggs of vipers and spin a spider's web. Whoever eats their eggs will die..." (Isaiah 59:4-5, NIV)

One must break the spider web of lies with the truth; and the truth will set you free. Then remove the spider.

Phil Bennett

"Spiritual Healing"

Copyright © Phil Bennett 2015
All rights reserved.

Special thanks to Jim Strong for the
Cover of the book, and
the many people who helped do
the Editing.

ISBN: 1508649634
ISBN 13: 9781508649632
Library of Congress Control Number: 2015903299
CreateSpace Independent Publishing Platform
North Charleston, South Carolina

Dedication

**THIS BOOK IS DEDICATED TO THE
GREATEST COUNSELOR THAT EXISTS,
THE HOLY SPIRIT.**

ALSO

My wife and ministry partner Janice Bennett
Two great men of God, My grandsons,
Jonathan Parker Bunn
Hudson Phillip Bunn
New Granddaughter Bunn on the way
Granddaughter Rachel Lee Grady

Foreword

SPIRITUAL HEALING

I like things that work. Don't get me wrong, as a fan of education, starting out with theory and philosophy are fine, as long as they funnel down into a workable plan that actually makes sense and, more importantly, gets results. In the NFL, offensive and defensive coordinators can watch film, theorize, and strategize, but at the end of the day, all of that theory needs to end up in a playbook that works.

Phil Bennett has written a playbook that works. For the past twelve years, I have watched first-hand how Phil has taught, counseled, and prayed countless people through to freedom from addictions, bondages, and all sorts of things the enemy uses to hold people back. I have had a front row seat to true miracles in our church as I have seen people healed physically, mentally, and emotionally by walking through the principles Phil teaches in this book. These are far more than just theory -they work.

Too many times prayer stops short of action and often our actions are void of the power of prayer. Phil Bennett has written a book that encourages and inspires both. The principles outlined in this book are reflective of the lifestyle of a true man of prayer. They will also lead you through practical steps of walking in obedience toward the goal of truly living free.

I am convinced that our people are better and our church is better for having sat under Phil's teaching ministry. I am convinced that you will be too. As you read these pages, I encourage you to read with prayerful obedience, and expect God to lift you to higher levels of freedom than you've ever experienced!

    Dr. Rick Ross
    Lead Pastor of Concord First Assembly
    Convoy of Hope Pastors National Committee Chairman
    Priority One Missions Board Member
    Assistant Superintendent of the North Carolina Assemblies of God

A Personal Testimony

I am a PK (Preacher's Kid). I grew up in the church. More importantly, I have been a follower of Jesus Christ for most of my life. I knew about spiritual oppression, but never thought it possible that an unclean spirit could attach itself to a true believer. I was wrong. While serving in one of the ministries of my local church, God started dealing with me in a way that I had never experienced before. He began speaking into my heart that I desperately needed him. I thought, Lord, I love you and have tried to serve you most of my life...of course I need you. But He kept speaking the same thing...that I desperately needed him. Then over the course of a few months, things began to go very wrong in my life. My job of 20+ years was threatened. Multiple family members experienced life threatening health conditions. My health too, suffered. I was drained...physically, emotionally, and spiritually. The enemy of my soul began spinning a web of lies that were hard to ignore...constantly telling me the worst was going to happen... because I was worthless and deserved it. I felt swallowed alive by unending fear. And with fear came defeat. It seemed no matter which way I turned, nothing got better. I never stopped believing or praying, but God felt a million miles away.

Then one night, the Holy Spirit showed me a vision. I saw a man from behind with what looked like a large insect attached to his back. I soon realized I was looking at myself. I struggled to remove what had attached itself to me, but because it was lodged into my flesh and on my back, I could not reach it. When I turned to the left it turned with me. And when I turned to the right, again it turned with me. I knew immediately this was the source of my torment...the spirit of fear incarnate. Over the days that followed, I knew what I had seen was very real...and I knew I needed help to dislodge this evil being that sought to drain me of peace, joy, and hope.

During this same time, I felt drawn to start attending Pastor Phil's class on Wednesday nights, and so my wife and I did just that. It seemed the only time I felt relief from the fear I was experiencing was when I was in class on Wednesdays. As a PK, I thought I had things pretty well figured out and seeking help or guidance from someone else had never been an option. I have come to know now that was also a lie spun by the enemy. Despite my reluctance, I made an appointment to speak with Pastor Phil.

We spoke for several minutes before I mustered the courage to share the vision I had seen and shared a similar picture with him. We talked, prayed, and I listened intently for the next two hours. The details of our discussion are not that important, but what is important is that Pastor Phil confirmed what we were dealing with. He explained that he too had dealt with fear...that God had delivered him...and that I could also be delivered. We prayed, believed together, and the Holy Spirit intervened...binding the strong man that had attached himself to me...and he had no choice but to let go his grasp that very hour! Oh he comes back around from time to time with the same lies and deceit that he has spun in the past, but I've come to recognize him for what he is. I know now just how desperately I need God...every day of my life...and instead of believing the false evidence the enemy wants to appear real, I choose instead to focus on the purest of love that God has for me and claim the victory that is mine as promised in 1 John 4:18, which says "Perfect love casts out all fear".

A Brother in Christ

Table of Contents

Dedication	iii
Foreword	v
A Personal Testimony	vii
Introduction	xi
Prologue	xv
1. The Spider Web Of Fear	1
2. The Spider Web Of Unforgiveness	15
3. Pornography, False Gods, Vain Imaginations And Other Spiders	27
4. The Need For Safe Boundaries From Any Web	37
5. Inner Healing And Deliverance From The Spider	45
6. Sustaining Freedom After Being Delivered From The Spider.	62
7. What Does A Healed Mind Look Like That Is Based On Christ?	74
Final Conclusion	85
Notes and References	89
About The Author	93

Introduction

SPIRITUAL HEALING FROM THE SPIDER WEB OF LIES
(Isaiah 59)

This work is not meant to be exhaustive in its scope of the healing of the mind, soul, and spirit but rather a useful manual for those in need of certain healings. A quick read that like a manual gives instruction one can follow to find new spiritual freedom. It's an encouragement for sure but also it works! I know it works because I learned from personal experience and by helping numbers of other people.

Do you need healing from fear, panic attacks, unforgiveness, loss of control, a need for boundaries in relationships, deliverance, and uncontrollable thoughts? Then perhaps this brief manual will teach you some things you can do and bring you more hope.

"Listen, the Lord's arm is not too weak to save you, nor is his ear too deaf to hear you call. It's your sins that have cut you off from God." (Isaiah 59:1-2, NIV) When the sin is uncovered then we can see to be saved. As we turn from the sin we find the long awaited for salvation. His arm can always reach us no matter where we are.

"...your lips are full of lies, and your mouth spews corruption." (Isaiah 59:3, NIV) We believe lies that corrupts us; but when the truth is finally known we can be set free.

"They conceive evil deeds and then give birth to sin. They hatch deadly snakes and weave spider's webs. Whoever falls into their webs will die, and there's danger even in getting near them. Their webs can't be made into clothing, and nothing they do is productive. All their activity is filled with sin, and violence is their trademark. "(Isaiah 59:4-6, NLT)

These spider webs are woven with lies as the Word just said. There is danger even getting near them, and if you fall into them you will die spiritually. You will be physically alive like an insect in a cobweb, but you are held and confined by a stronghold unable to be free.

The webs in the mind are built "...on empty arguments, they utter lies, they conceive trouble and give birth to evil. "(Isaiah 59:4, NIV). These arguments are empty of truth, but still believed. Once the enemy has won the battle in your mind he can get your body to do anything he wants as quoted in the Word.

"Their deeds are evil deeds," v.6
"Their feet rush into sin;" v.7
"They pursue evil schemes;" v.7
"The way of peace they do not know;"v.8

You'll find out in the last chapter that the way of peace is a life we can all enjoy!

The problem comes by what we believe at first. We believe the lie and then we just do what comes natural in the flesh after that. We accept it as normal and believe it cannot be changed. Our flesh or our old man must be removed and replaced with a new man that thinks differently.

It's only when a person knows the truth that the truth can release them from captivity. This book encourages a person to pursue the truth that can then replace the lies freeing one to live a better life.

The Bible says our enemy "...was a murderer from the beginning, and does not stand for the truth; because there is no truth in him." (John 8:44, AMP) Since he has no truth in him; he is spiritually dead and seeks the same fate for everyone else. "...when he tells a lie, he is speaking in character: because he is a liar— indeed the inventor of the lie! (John 8: 44, CJB)

The enemy is like a spider who invents lies to spin his web of deceit spinning even the truth at times into a lie. We get the word wicked from a wick that is made by being twisted. The enemy only has to carefully weave a lie even between two truths to twist the meaning in such a way that it becomes untruthful. A master of deception.

> "satan, however is as subtle as God is good,
> and he tries to counterfeit everything God does,
> and if he cannot counterfeit it, he will limit it.
> Do not be ignorant of his devices."
> (Oswald Chambers)

It's my goal to pass on to you things I have learned that works in an easy to read manual so you will no longer be ignorant of the spider and his webs of lies. You will know what to do. You will then be able to grow spiritually as you learn to overcome and trust the Holy Spirit to guide you. You will build a working relationship with the Spirit of God and He will lead you into truths that will bring you a new freedom.

A <u>KEY</u> is to learn how to train your mind to start reading your thoughts. To listen to what is being said to you. To stop accepting limitations you've always accepted about yourself. You will learn to discern what is truth, what is of God and what isn't. This is very important and you will need the Spirit of God to help you discern that. You will then need to cast

down false arguments you have always accepted that are not of God. When you repent or turn from false, evil arguments you've always accepted as a part of you-then you are on a pathway to a new exciting self.

Living free in Christ will require you to always maintain a vigil over what you are thinking or hearing what is being said to you. One discerns by watching and praying and studying the Word to enable discernment needed to dismiss what is lies and believe only truth. The goal is to remove the spider and the webs he has spun in your life. Knowing how is the mission of this book.

It is said that Reverend Billy Graham tells of a time early in his ministry when he arrived in a small town to preach a sermon. Wanting to mail a letter, he asked a young boy where the post office was. When the boy had told him, Dr. Graham thanked him and said, "If you'll come to the Baptist Church this evening, you can hear me telling everyone how to get to heaven."

"The boy replied, "I don't think I'll be there... You don't even know your way to the post office."

God will show us the way and I will share what He has shown me that works.

There are certain webs the enemy favors in order to destroy people spiritually. We are addressing ones used often for both believers and non-believers to bring them into captivity. They are fear, unforgiveness, need for boundaries, false idols and vain imaginations. Also discussed are how to be delivered from these captivities, how to sustain your new freedom while learning how to live free in Christ. Everyone can be set free. In addition, we will learn that one can also have a spiritually healthy mind that is available to everyone in Christ.

Prologue

The foundational concept for this manual to work in your life is the following belief.

Lies are powerful and usually hidden

A lie is as powerful as the truth if you believe it. It will block your life from moving forward. An example of how powerful a lie can be is when Roger Banister, a track star, broke the four-minute mile in 1954. I heard that German scientists said at the time that it was humanly impossible to run faster. The human body was just not engineered to do it. Everyone believed the lie so no one broke the record. After Roger broke the record, it only took 46 days for another person to break it, because then people knew it could be done. The barrier that was holding everyone back was only a lie; it had finally been uncovered.

Another example of a lie that created a huge barrier was the lie that the world was flat. People were afraid to go out on the open seas and challenge it. Christopher Columbus challenged the lie and discovered a whole new world.

We also discover a whole new world opening before us once we learn not to be held back by lies. Spiritual strongholds are built by lies that hold us like a spider web; and makes us believe we can't break free even though we can.

**Some common lies people believe are:
I will always be a fearful person.
I will never lose weight.
I can't quit smoking.
I will never be able to forgive that person for what they did.**

A characteristic of a stronghold is the belief that it can't be broken because they've tried in the past unsuccessfully. That it can't be broken is a lie from the enemy. The lies build arguments the person accepts. The Bible says we are to cast down all arguments set against the truth of God's word that blocks the knowledge we could have of God.

The Bible contradicts the lie we can't do it. It says, " I can do all things through Christ which strengthened me." (Philippians 4:13, KJV) This book is meant to encourage you to take God up on His promise that with His help there is nothing you can't do. We may know we have the means in Christ but not know how to work with Him to accomplish it.

The spider webs can easily be broken, once one knows how. Knowing how is the purpose of this book. Like Columbus whole new worlds are awaiting those who find this truth.

Spiritual Healing

The Spider Web Of Lies

Scripture
(ISAIAH 59:1-20, NIV)
[We long for light, but sink into darkness]
"Surely the arm of the Lord is not too short
to save, nor his ear too dull to hear.
But your iniquities have separated you from your God; your
sins have hidden his face from you so that he will not hear.
For your hands are stained with blood,
your fingers with guilt.
Your lips have spoken falsely, and your
tongue mutters wicked things.
No one calls for justice; no one pleads a case with integrity.
They rely on empty arguments, they utter lies;
they conceive trouble and give birth to evil.
They hatch the eggs of vipers and spin a
Spider's web.
Whoever eats their eggs will die, and when
one is broken, an adder is hatched.
Their cobwebs are useless for clothing; they cannot
cover themselves with what they make.
Their deeds are evil deeds, and acts of
violence are in their hands,
Their feet rush into sin; they are swift to shed innocent blood.
They pursue evil schemes; acts of violence mark their ways.
The way of peace they do not know; there
is no justice in their paths.
They have turned them into crooked roads; no
one who walks along them will know peace.
So justice is far from us, and righteousness does not reach us.
We look for light, but all is darkness;
for brightness, but we walk in deep shadows.
Like the blind we grope along the wall,
feeling our way like people without eyes.

PHIL BENNETT

*At midday we stumble as if it were twilight;
among the strong, we are like the dead.
We all growl like bears; we moan mournfully like doves.
We look for justice, but find none; for
deliverance, but it is far away.
For our offenses are many in your sight,
and our sins testify against us.
Our offenses are ever with us, and we acknowledge
our iniquities: rebellion and treachery against the
Lord, turning our backs on our God, inciting revolt and
oppression, uttering lies our hearts have conceived.
So justice is driven back, and righteousness
stands at a distance; truth has stumbled in
the streets, honesty cannot enter.
Truth is nowhere to be found, and whoever
shuns evil becomes a prey.
The Lord looked and was displeased
that there was no justice.
He saw that there was no one, he was appalled that there
was no one to intervene; so his own arm achieved salvation
for him, and his own righteousness sustained him. He put on
righteousness as his breastplate, and the
helmet of salvation on his head; he put on the garments
of vengeance and wrapped himself in zeal as in a cloak.
According to what they have done, so he will
repay wrath to his enemies and retribution to
his foes; he will repay the islands their due.
From the west, people will fear the name of the Lord, and
from the rising of the sun, they will revere his glory.
For he will come like a pent-up flood that
the breath of the Lord drives along.
The Redeemer will come to Zion, to those in Jacob who repent
of their sins," declares the Lord." (Isaiah 59:1-20, NIV)*

The lies of the enemy that we accept in our mind spins a web that creates a hold on us and keeps us from realizing the potential of who we really are in Christ. The Bible tells us how to break strongholds in our mind:

"The weapons we fight with are not the weapons of the world. On the contrary, they have divine power to demolish strongholds. We demolish arguments, and every pretension that sets itself up against the knowledge of God, and we take captive every thought to make it obedient to Christ." (2 Corinthians 10: 4-5, NIV)

The word pretension is used because the enemy pretends to speak the truth when using lies to block our knowledge of God. That's why when you replace lies with truth you discover a new freedom in Christ; and also grow in Christ to a new level.

When you learn how to do this you will be able to demolish the strongholds- the spider web itself. It's also important to then remove the spider or enemy of Christ that constructed it. The old door must not be left open for a spider to reconstruct another spider web. But if you only remove the spider, the web or your old way of thinking will remain the same. It's important to remove both the spider web and the spider.

God does not make it hard for us to use His weapons and they always work. Learn how so you can pick up the weapons and use them not once but daily to live in a new world of freedom.

We must learn to see the **dashboard** of our mind to read what we are thinking, and capture the lies and cast down the arguments against the truth of the knowledge of God.

God promises, if we confess our sins He is always faithful to forgive us. Adam and Eve sinned and hid their sin because they were ashamed.

Our enemy the spider is banking on that because if we hide our sin instead of bringing it to God then we cannot receive forgiveness. It is important to be open with God so He can show us how to repent or turn away from the sin and not be caught in it's never-ending web. The Bible cautions us if we do not handle sin properly. "And if you do not do well, sin lies at the door. And its desire is for you, but you should rule over it." (Gen.4: 7, NKJV). The spider waits at the door ready to catch you in a web to be held captive. However, this book is written that you might know how to be free and actually rule over it.

"In this way, He disarmed the spiritual rulers and authorities. He shamed them publicly by His victory over them on the cross." (Colossians 2:15, NLT)

~Choose a chapter you want to do some spiritual work in and get started with the knowledge Christ has already won the victory for you.~

1

THE SPIDER WEB OF FEAR

"we look for light but all is darkness" (Isaiah 59:9, NIV)
Fear is the opposite of love, power, and a sound mind. We do not have any of these three when we have fear— only darkness.

Fear brings dark ominous, foreboding feelings. I know I lived with fear until I was in my 20's. It would come in waves and brought an oppression that dominated my thoughts and sometimes paralyzed me so that I seemingly couldn't move past it. Sometimes it brought a chill down my back. At other times, I'd feel warmth come over me which was not a nice, warm, fuzzy experience, but very uncomfortable. I had been saved and a born again child of God since I was a child. I asked God to remove it but He didn't. I thought it was just my personality since it always seemed to be a part of my life.

Then one of the greatest days of my life occurred. I was in my office when I received a threat against the business I was in at the time. Then a wave came in with dark ominous thoughts of everything bad that could happen. None of it did; but if you don't know how to stop the thoughts, then they can take over your mind. The physical feelings came as I was all heated up, feeling alone in that darkness isolated and afraid. I was in a web of fear.

The only thing I had learned to do was to walk around and pray crying out to God and eventually it would subside. I never put together that it was something coming against me. A still small voice said, "How long are you going to put up with that, Phillip (He always calls me Phillip; though no one else does). He said, "that's the enemy!"
I said "that's the enemy I always thought that was an inherit weakness on my part." He said, "No! That's the enemy." Well I knew I didn't have to put up with him, that Christ had already won the victory over him. So, I decided right then not to put up with him anymore. I prayed and a scripture came to mind I didn't realize I knew; and I prayed it.

"I asked for God's perfect love to come into me and cast out all fear."
(the complete Scripture is found in 1 John 4:18)
When I said that prayer I felt something like a cool refreshing shower come over me from the top of my head going all the way down and out my feet. It wasn't until later that I realized something was coming in; but also something was going out. I used God's weapon His Word; and the spider or enemy was removed from me. Wow ! I was not possessed but oppressed by the enemy of my soul.

Then I received some more instruction from the Lord. The enemy, "the one oppressing you and hooked inside you is now out; but you must keep him out. You must not let the thoughts of fear come into your mind that builds a web or stronghold in your mind. It will create a habitat for the enemy, the spider, to move in and out of."

I started learning how the enemy could work inside my mind; even though I was not possessed by him, he still could control parts of my thinking if I let him. He then could make my life miserable. I needed to learn how to keep him out. However, he was ruling me with fear in areas of my life through my mind.

The Lord taught me when you are thinking of thoughts that make you afraid; and all those dark feelings start to come then immediately capture those thoughts. Then ask Me your savior to take them away- I did and it worked. I then came to an agreement with the Lord:

FROM NOW ON "ZERO TOLERANCE FOR FEAR"

My whole life was changed once I learned how to use these weapons of God. I cannot begin to tell you how much I changed! I lost a lot of anger. I learned anger is the second emotion; it stems from fear that is the first emotion. When the fear was gone so went a lot of anger. When I used to try to do things that were so often defeated, I could now push through them and succeed. More peace was in my life and I began to relax more and enter God's rest. The constant nervousness I always felt was dissipating.

THE SIXTY SECOND RULE

I learned the 60-second rule. Whenever the wave of negative thoughts came, I would capture those thoughts and ask God to remove them. However, they didn't leave right away and I thought it wasn't working until I learned what I call the 60-second rule. It only took 5-10 seconds to ask God to remove the thoughts. Then I would start thanking him for delivering me from fear and by the time I hit 60 seconds it was over. The enemy only keeps doing things that work and this wasn't working for him anymore. Thank God!

Do I hear an amen? When the spider web of fear was broken I learned I could be concerned about something; but no longer had to live with fear. The spider was removed and the door he was using to get me to fear was finally closed. I asked God to remove the spider— in this case the spirit of fear and He did.

"For God has not given us the spirit of fear; but of power, and of love and of a sound mind." (2 Timothy 1: 7, NKJV).

Again God does not give us a spirit of fear; but He gives us the opposite: love, power, and a sound mind. We don't have any of those three when we have fear.

<u>You Have either:</u>

FEAR   OR   LOVE
POWER
SOUND MIND

The person gripped by fear does not feel loved, does not have power, but has only a feeling of being weak and is not thinking soundly. They may be locked up and not have any idea what to do next.

I found that the fear that was dominating my life was a spirit. When I began to see it was an intelligent being that was coming against me, then it all began to make sense. When I felt the chills or the heat that was attached to the thoughts and feelings, I realized that it was a thing attacking me. I decided since I knew Christ I didn't have to put up with it.

I even repented and asked God to forgive me for spending so much time with His enemy. I was Christ's bride and was spending a lot of time thinking and feeling things concerning fear. I learned that fear is the point man seeking anyone who will buy into what he is selling and spinning. If he gets into your mind he can bring rage, terror, anger, frustration and a lack of peace. Lack of peace will block spending quality time listening and being renewed with the Lord.

What I have written below has helped me a lot. I copied it and at the time placed it on my mirror at home and on the dashboard of my car.

I did that so I could remember this truth: that most of what we fear NEVER HAPPENS.

FEAR IS:

F alse
E vidence
A ppearing
R eal

Fear is False Evidence Appearing Real. It looks like something we should be worried about; but it never happens. Even the secular world knows that. It knows that for some reason 80-90% of what we worry about doesn't happen. They have no biblical teaching to put together that there may be someone putting those thoughts in their mind. People do not naturally desire thoughts of fear, worry and anxiety. They are imported into our minds.

How do we keep them out? By learning to listen to what is being said to us. Sometimes it's us speaking the wrong things to ourselves or it's other individuals. A lot of the time it's the enemy of our soul seeking whom he may control or devour.

The Holy Spirit will help us flag those thoughts we should capture and then we can submit them to the truth of God's word. When the thoughts are not of him then ask him to delete them from our mind. You can learn to do that quickly and easily accomplishing more and more spiritual freedom.

"For those who are led by the Spirit of God are the children of God. The Spirit you received does not make you slaves, so that you live in fear again; rather, the Spirit you received brought about your adoption to sonship. And by him we cry, Abba Father." (Romans 8: 15, NIV). One spirit you can receive will make you a slave to fear, the other will set you free. You can receive in your flesh bondage built in your own mind to fear along with an evil spirit oppressing you in fear. But both are overcome by the Holy Spirit who can bring you freedom from fear by trusting Him and His love to keep you safe as your defender.

Set the spider trap by capturing thoughts

Learning this helps to keep us from enduring more spider webs that will need to be broken. To break the web or stronghold we need to read or listen to our thoughts. What are the thoughts and then what does God want us to see and understand. We very often do not live with the facts but only the story we told ourselves about the facts. Because we live with distorted views of the facts, we often live with lies and not truth.

Sometimes we are living with a lie believed in childhood that now perverts what we still will believe. For example, a grown middle aged woman was told as a little girl being molested that this is what she was created for and she should submit. Another adult female, in a similar situation as a child was told she was dirty and evil and that she was the one causing it to happen. These lies become hidden and actually became a part of the person's life and belief system. Once the lies are exposed, then you can help the person declare the truth. It is remarkable how their life is changed. They discover they are clean and beautiful in Christ.

As a pastor when ministering to people I ask them to make declarations out loud defining the lie from the truth. I explain that words are powerful as they can speak life and death into us. Once we believe the lie we keep telling ourselves it's the truth and it becomes a false truth. Our own thinking then holds us in a web. The spider actually no longer has to tell us the lies we have them programed into the software of our mind.

So we need to capture the thoughts (the source of the virus), quarantine it like a computer does, and then delete it. In this way, our mind or software can operate properly. When the spider's lies are in operation, our thinking becomes flawed, confused and slows us down because our software is contaminated. So we must identify the virus/lies- capturing them and deleting them with the Holy Spirit's help. Otherwise, like a computer, we can get locked up by a powerful virus.

We can learn and integrate what the Bible says so it will renew or reprogram our minds. We replace the old way of thinking with a new way. We do that by making declarations of truth and keep making those declarations so the new reprogrammed man, crafted by God, can be in control.

Therefore using the above examples I would ask the person to repeat this prayer declaring it before God for them and for any enemy of their soul in earshot to hear.

"I was not created evil. I may have done some evil things but I am not evil. The truth is that I am now a child of God who has been cleansed of all evil.

I was not created to do improper things because people want me to. I am not dirty but cleansed by the blood of Jesus. I have the right to say NO to people who want to hurt me."

Sigmund Freud the father of modern psychology believed once you knew the cause, then you would be healed. Not so. A person may know that when someone pushed them out of barn loft and broke their arm – that's when the fear of heights came in. That doesn't mean they are now cured. You have to know what to do with that information. One must declare the truth that when they are in a high place now they can be sure that no one is around who would push them. They are safe now and no longer have to fear what once happened. Then with God's help, they can step onto a balcony and know that God is with them. They need not fear any longer. They undo the lie with what they know now is the truth.

Learn to live free of fear

We can actually live free of fear and its dark foreboding feelings. We give ourselves permission to be concerned about the danger of driving; but we do not live in fear of those dangers. I've had people come into my office with their hands shaking and afraid to return to work where they were being bullied. People suffering panic attacks while shopping in the grocery store can be free of every fear.

One technique I've found to help people is just to simply write down what things they have fear about at the moment. They believe it is a long list; it is always a short list.

Then ask them what is the worst thing that could happen in each case. It turns out that often it can be resolved. Many say the worst that can happen is to die in which case they will be with the Lord and free of all pain in this world. However, God is using these trials to help them grow spiritually and having lived through them they will be stronger not weaker.

What I have found is that the trials always are there as Peter said, " Don't think it strange to have trials." However, I need God to expand me from within to meet the pressure coming against me. I have learned God will comfort me and give me His peace that sustains me while I wait and work on a new challenge. I know He will not allow any trial too great for me and will actually use it to help me grow. Since He is in control I don't have to be. I've learned I can enter His rest and relax in the midst of any challenge that comes my way. He will truly work it together for my own good when I am committed to Him.

There was a quote in a Billy Graham Evangelism mailing in January 2014 that said, "An estimated 40 million people in the US feel trapped or crippled by fear. They live as prisoners to their own anxiety." It's believed fear in its basic form results from an effort to avoid pain. Most of what we are trying to avoid is the pain of something while living in the fear of it. We do not need to avoid what God has placed before us; because we know he has already made a way for us. We are not allowed to fear only trust.

"The spider skillfully grasps with its hands, and it is in kings' palaces." (Proverbs 30:28,NKJV). The spider takes hold and attacks our will, so we will not even try to escape no matter whom we may be or what palace we live in. He attempts to take our hope away. Without hope we lose heart. "Whose hope shall be cut off, and whose trust [shall be] a spider's web." (Job 8:14, KJV). When we do not trust God, we fall into the spider's web of deception.

THE WORLD FEARS

"According to psychiatric reference books, there are approximately two thousand classified fears. Those documented fears run the gamut-everything from triskaidekaphobia (the fear of the number 13) to arachibutyrophobia (the fear of peanut butter sticking to the roof of your mouth). There is even a phobophobia – the fear of acquiring a phobia.
What's interesting is that psychiatrist's say that we are born with only two innate fears: the fear of falling and fear of loud noises.
That means that every other fear is learned. And more importantly that means that every other fear can be unlearned." (Mark Batterson).

There is hope for everyone who fears. It can be unlearned just as it was learned. Once the fear is discovered we can then replace it with the truth of God's Word. "There is no fear in love. But (God's) perfect love drives out fear." (1John 4:18, NIV). The goal of God's love is to make you fearless, that is, without fear.

The Bible says, "Fear not, for I am with you; be not dismayed, for I am your God. I will strengthen you, yes, I will help you." (Isaiah 41:10, NKJV).

We must as an act of our will, say I refuse to fear. Instead I commit it to God, whom I know has always gotten me through every situation in the past. Therefore, I just rest in in His strength. A person can know that even in death they will have victory.

How can they know they have victory? They can know it by confessing they're a sinner like everyone else and asking Jesus to forgive you. If they mean it in their heart, they can know He means it when He said that he would not only forgive them, but also cleanse them of every sin. He cleanses you just as if you never have sinned. Invite God to be your friend and partner in life forever.

"If we say that we have no sin, we deceive ourselves, and the truth is not in us.

If we confess our sins, He is faithful and just to forgive us our sins and to cleanse us from all unrighteousness." (1John 1: 8-9 NKJV).

Simply declare right now this truth:
"LORD I CONFESS I HAVE SINNED AND ASK YOU TO FORGIVE AND CLEANSE ME."

"I BELIEVE IN FAITH THAT WHAT YOUR WORD SAYS IS TRUE. THAT YOU WILL FORGIVE ME AND CLEANSE ME OF EVERY SIN. THANK YOU FOR DOING THAT RIGHT NOW."

Now nothing is separating you from God; you and Him can work through anything together.

The past is covered by His BLOOD, which has washed you clean of all sins. The future is in His hands, so now you can enjoy this present moment. It's a gift only God can give—a present— whereby you can enjoy your life in the now.

If there are over 2000 classified fears there is probably a spider attached to each one. God's goal for us is not to live with any of them but to live with Him who loves us and has the power to deliver us. We can live spider free.

I'm told there are over 365 "fear not's", "don't be afraid", etc. in the Bible— one for each day. God knew a spider would be on the prowl daily to attach itself to a person.

He can only crawl through a door of deception. Once one is aware of the falsehoods, the spider or thief is exposed, and the bandit of joy and peace can be removed.

Jesus said He was sent "to proclaim liberty to the captives"(Isaiah 61:1, NKJV). Fear holds one captive.

Max Lucado, in his book the "Applause of Heaven" discussed the "Bandit of Joy." "He was a professional thief. His name stirred fear as the desert wind stirs tumbleweeds. He terrorized the Wells Fargo stage line for 13 years, roaring like a tornado in and out of the Sierra Nevada's, spooking the most rugged frontiersman. In journals from San Francisco to New York, his name became synonymous with the danger of the frontier.

During his reign of terror between 1875 and 1883, he is credited with stealing the bags and the breath away from 29 different stagecoach crews. And he did it all without firing a shot.

His weapon was his reputation. His ammunition was intimidation.

A hood hid his face. No victim ever saw him. No artist ever sketched his features. No Sheriff could ever track his trail.

His name was Black Bart; but once the hood was off He turned out to be nothing to fear. He was found to be a meek druggist from Decatur, Illinois.

"The man the papers pictured storming through the mountains on horseback was, in reality, so afraid of the horses he rode to and from the robberies in a buggy. He was Charles E. Boles, the bandit, who never once fired a shot because he never once loaded his gun."

The enemy of our soul is a hidden dark evil that must work through deception because he was defeated at the cross of Cavalry. He is still effective to the one who is deceived and will believe his lies.

"Perfect love drives out fear, because fear has to do with punishment (or torment)." (1John 4:18, NIV). God's perfect love means you trust him to keep you safe.

The people of the Sierra Nevada's never suspected that Black Bart was only Charles Boles who never fired a shot. The people of the world know most of what we worry about never happens but they do not know the source of the lies and they often take the bait that it must be true.

"The remarkable thing about fearing God is that when you fear God you fear nothing else, whereas if you do not fear God you fear everything else." (Oswald Chambers).

READ YOUR DASHBOARD

Learn to read your dashboard when you start heating up. Just like with your car pull over, deal with your problem so you don't lose the life of your car or yourself. When the dark ominous feelings come, immediately stop, capture those thoughts and submit them to Christ that He might delete the lies. The few things that may turn out to be of real concern are given over to God to carry for us. We win no matter what- when we give everything to the Lord.

**~"I sought the Lord, and he answered me and delivered me from all my fears."~
(Psalm 34:4 ESV).**

SUMMARY

**We are created to live free!
What then should we remember to do?**

Read the dashboard of your mind and be aware of the thoughts you're thinking. If you are thinking fearful thoughts then you know you are not allowed to fear and most of those are lies anyway. God will take care of any concerns that turn out to be true by simply trusting Him. You are commanded not to fear so tell yourself you are not allowed to.

Capture every fearful thought and ask God to delete it. Each time ask God to pour His perfect love into you and cast out all fear.

Make a declaration of "Zero Tolerance for Fear" You are not allowed to live with it.

The "Sixty Second Rule" —remember it may take up to 60 seconds for the Lord to respond and remove the enemy coming against you. Fill those seconds with praise for God's deliverance.

Tell yourself the truth, odds are it's only Charles Boles and not Black Bart.

Scriptures on fear to pray with and be comforted (Over 100 verses of fear not or don't be afraid in the bible.

"He delivered me from my strong enemy, from those who hated me, for they were too strong for me. They confronted me in the day of my calamity, but the lord was my support." (Psalm 18:17-18, NKJV).

"...do not be afraid, for I am with you and will bless you." (Genesis 26:24, NLT).

"Do not be afraid or discouraged, for the lord will personally go ahead of you. He will be with you; he will neither fail you nor abandon you." (Deuteronomy. 31:8, NLT)

"The lord is my light and my salvation—so why should I be afraid? The Lord is my fortress, protecting me from danger, so why should I tremble."(Psalm 27:1, NLT).

"For He will rescue you from every trap and protect you from deadly disease. He will cover you with His feathers. He will shelter you with His wings. His faithful promises are your armor and protection." (Psalm 91:3-4, NLT)

"So you have not received a spirit that makes you fearful slaves. Instead, you received God's spirit when he adopted you as his own children. Now we call him, Abba father." (Romans 8:15, NLT).

"For God has not given us a spirit of fear, but of power and of love and of a sound mind." (2 Timonthy.1: 7, NKJV).

"Such love has no fear, because perfect love expels all fear. If we are afraid, it is for fear of punishment, and this shows that we have not fully experienced his perfect love."(1 John 4:18, NLT).

2

The Spider Web Of Unforgiveness

*"Rebellion and treachery against the Lord;
turning our backs on our God."
(Isaiah 59:13, NIV).
Unforgiveness is rebellion against God. When
we forgive, it brings healing to us.*

I've heard it said that you could empty out 80% of the counseling centers if people could only learn to forgive those who have hurt them in the past. Why is that?

God commanded us to forgive others, if we expect to be forgiven. That's huge!

"For if you forgive other people when they sin against you, your heavenly Father will also forgive you. But if you do not forgive others their sins, your Father will not forgive your sins." (Matthew 6:14-15, NIV).

I don't think Christians think about what that means if they refuse to forgive other people, then the Father will not forgive them. I've seen Christians brag about how they will get even with the one who hurt them. They are never thinking that if they don't forgive others, then they are putting at risk the Father forgiving them.

FORGIVING IS NOT AN OPTION

Some will say you don't know what they have done to me how they have hurt me!

How can I ever forgive them? You can forgive their offense because the Father has forgiven you all your sins. Otherwise, you bear the fruit of carrying the offense: the feelings of hurt, bitterness, pain, betrayal, depression, rage, frustration, and more spiritual bondage.

Another reason for you to forgive another who has brought an offense against you is because it is the only way you will ever heal from the effects of the wrong. Your healing comes through a pathway of forgiveness. It will not come through revenge. God said that "vengeance is Mine" because He knew He did not create us to carry revenge. We can't carry it and remain healthy, but He can deal with it in the fairest way. Our soul is not constructed by the creator to survive unforgiveness and revenge without cold hardened spiritual death creeping into our inner being. We live in bitterness in unfulfilled revenge.

"Bear with each other and forgive one another if any of you has a grievance against someone. Forgive as the Lord forgave you." (Colossians 3:13,NIV).

How does the Lord forgive us? Immediately. The quicker we forgive, the quicker we can move on with our life. Forgiving others is not for their sake. They may not even know or care if we have forgiven them. It's for our benefit that we forgive them following Christ example who forgave all who hurt Him.

We think if we withhold our forgiveness, we are punishing them. They don't even know many times how we feel about them. It will destroy us and the enemy of our soul knows it. He even baits us into being offended with others. We cannot stop offenses from coming, but our goal is to not accept the offense and become offended. **"It is impossible that no offenses should come,.."** **(Luke 17:1, NKJV).**

Offenses are coming! But when we do not stop and deal with them right away, the enemy will start spinning a new web.

That web could separate me from the Father and my salvation. It is not something to play with. So watch the **dashboard** of your mind and recognize any thoughts of unforgiveness.

It is not as hard to forgive when you know what will happen if you don't. The spider is hoping you will give into your flesh and want to get even. If you give into it you will start to be filled with hate, anger rage, jealousy, envy strife, bitterness, betrayal, and more. That's quite a price for you to pay for something someone else did and not you. People do not realize how much they are letting other people control them by picking up an offense from them.

They sometimes think by withholding forgiveness they are punishing the other person.

Most of the time the other person does not even know they are holding a grudge.

Resist the spider's trap

The quicker you can release the offense the better even while it's occurring. Stop the spider from getting in as he starts spinning all the reasons you should be offended.

Here is how the spider spins his lies and establishes gates of hell around them:

If you forgive them then you're saying what they did was right. No, you are probably right and they are probably wrong that is not the issue. The issue is obeying God and trusting that he will get even; we are to forgive so we can be healed from the effects of it. We may have to call the police on a neighbor to stop them from stealing from us but to heal from the betrayal of their acts, we need to forgive them. Let the civil law deal with their punishment. When we release forgiveness, we let go the negative feelings we feel about it.

If I forgive them, I'm letting them off the hook with God. No! They are still held accountable by God for all their actions. That is between them and God.

I don't feel like forgiving them. Whether you feel like forgiving them or not isn't the issue; being obedient to God is. Start by saying as quickly as you can "I forgive them" just as Christ did while He was still on the cross. Some people feel like it's not sincere if you don't feel good about forgiving them. Take the step of faith and just do it whether you feel like it or not trusting the Lord.

Remember this is not about winning an argument. It's about what it's doing to you and your need to heal. It's not about who is right. You gave up your right to hold a grudge against another when you became a follower of Christ. You can then live in peace and love and not let others so easily control you with offenses.

You will rob the spider of a new web to control you. Remember the command, "Repay no one evil for evil." (Romans 12:17, NKJV).

WE ARE COMMANDED TO FORGIVE

"We may talk as much as we like about forgiveness, but it will never make any difference to us unless we realize that we need it. God can never forgive the man who does not want to be forgiven." (Oswald Chambers) A person you may need to forgive is yourself on a regular basis. I do it often as God brings to my mind things I should forgive myself for as He has already forgiven me. It brings a new level of healing every time. You are required to forgive yourself just as much as anyone else. It doesn't matter

SPIRITUAL HEALING

if you knew better. It matters that you receive your forgiveness Christ won for you on the cross so you can move on.

Some believe you should go to another you have offended, and ask their forgiveness. God might lead you to do that. However, I believe, with a repentant heart, you can ask God for forgiveness and receive your healing.

PRAYER OF FORGIVENESS
When others have brought an offense against us.

Example, "Father I forgive this man for stealing from me. Not because what he did was right, because it wasn't. Not because I feel like it; you know I don't feel like doing this. Not because I'm letting him off the hook with you as he's still held accountable by you. But, as an act of my will and for my healing I say- **"I forgive him"**.
I ask you now to pour your perfect love into me and let it flow to this person flushing out all bitterness, hurt, and pain I feel. I will not let what they did fill me with pain and suffering. I want to do this God's way so He can heal me."

If I don't forgive them then I am willfully violating the two greatest commandments to love God and to love my fellow man.

UNFORGIVENESS IS NOT AN OPTION
Unforgiveness will ultimately separate me from God and my prayer life will be interrupted because of my willful disobedience. My ministry and ability to flow in God's love is interrupted.
I will lose power to minister on God's behalf because I am in conflict with Him.
The spider web that is spun and continues to be spun affecting every relationship I have.
I will become bound by the person who brought the offense even if I'm no longer around them.

For example in the O J Simpson murder case, the father of the son who was killed brought his own suit against O J Simpson. Even though he won, he still tracked Simpson around the country not letting him write a book to make money years later.

He did not get closure in court; Simpson still binds him.

On the other hand, the Amish in Pennsylvania forgave a man who killed their innocent children. This man went into an Amish schoolhouse and shot and killed their children. The Amish did not approve of the crime but forgave in obedience to God, and were cleansed of all the hurt and pain. The Amish grace was extended to the widow of the man who killed their children and then killed himself. It won the attention of the whole world making a statement of the power of forgiveness.

The Amish knew what to do immediately so the healing process began right away. Don't wait until after you've accepted the offense but immediately resist your flesh and the enemy (spider) at the outset.

"Resist him (satan/spider), standing firm in the faith, because you know that the family of believers throughout the world is undergoing the same kind of sufferings." (1Peter 5:9, NIV).

What others meant for harm and evil, God will work together for good. We will not just endure the trial but grow from it.

Once you have learned to forgive a current offense- then continue to forgive that offense every time it comes to mind to maintain the healing. Eventually it will fade away.

Asking God to pour His perfect love into you and letting it flow to the person who brought the offense will flush out all the toxic feelings.

This is a choice that works keeping the commitment to forgive every time the thought of the offense comes. Everyone can do this as God has enabled each of us to control our thoughts. Freedom comes, as the offense is put down, God's love is requested to come in and healing results.

The more we can forgive, the happier we are and the closer God draws to us in love.

"Forgive us our debts, as we also have forgiven our debtors."(Matt.6:12, NIV).

As we quickly and more thoroughly forgive others, then God forgives us in the same way.

LET US REVIEW WHAT TO DO WHEN AN OFFENSE COMES. REMEMBERING THE BIBLE TEACHES US THEY WILL ALWAYS COME.

*You give up your right to hold a grudge. Jesus commands us to forgive others if we expect to be forgiven.

*You forgive as an act of your will. You're not saying they deserve it any more than you deserve being forgiven for all your sins by God.

*You're not saying you feel like forgiving them because you probably don't.

*You're not letting them off the hook with God. They are still accountable to God for their wrongs.

What do you do then?

-Say verbally before God as an act of your will that you forgive the person for the offense.

-Continue to forgive them every time the offense arises in your mind again.

-Ask for God's love, as you may not have any love for the person, to be poured into your heart for the person flushing out all the toxic feelings you have inside for them.

This will cleanse your heart and mind freeing you to be healed and set free from the effects of the offense.

You will grow in this ability to more quickly be set free from the offenses brought by others. You will not be as easily controlled by others as a result of their actions toward you. Your relationship with the Lord will be greatly enhanced as you are obeying Him.

Some quotes on Forgiveness

"Forgiveness is not an occasional act, it is a constant attitude."
– Martin Luther King Jr.

"To forgive is the highest, most beautiful form of love. In return, you will receive untold peace and happiness"
– Robert Muller

"As I walked out the door toward the gate that would lead to my freedom, I knew if I didn't leave my bitterness and hatred behind, I'd still be in prison."
– Nelson Mandela

Most people are not aware that love is a tremendous spiritual weapon against unforgiveness. It is hard to hold a grudge against someone when you are praying for him or her and asking God to love him or her through you. It's engaging your enemy who seeks to make you unhappy and distraught the rest of your life. You are engaging in spiritual warfare when you obey God and love your fellow man.

"Beloved, never avenge yourselves, but leave the way open for [God's] wrath; for it is written, Vengeance is Mine, I will repay (requite), says the Lord." (Romans 12:19, Amplified).

Finally God has commanded us to leave any vengeance in His hands. I believe he does that because He knows He never created us to be able to handle that. We get very strange and filled with rage when we try to repay someone evil for the evil they have done. God can do a better job of revenge than we ever could and it will be fair the way we would want it for ourselves. God promises to strengthen us to release the offense.

> "...For I am your God. I will strengthen and harden you [to difficulties]; yes, I will help you; yes I will hold you up and retain you with my victorious right hand of rightness and justice. Behold all they who are enraged and inflamed against you shall be put to shame and confounded; they who strive against you shall be as nothing and shall perish. You shall seek for those who contend with you, and shall not find them; they who war against you shall be as nothing, as nothing at all. For I, the Lord your God, hold your right hand; I, who say to you Fear not, I will help you!"(Isaiah 41:10-13, Amplified).

One can begin to see that when you are in God's will, he will repay strengthen us to endure the challenge, and remove our enemies. Let Him do the fighting and we do the forgiving.

> "Hatred is the rabid dog that turns on you.
> Revenge is the raging fire that consumes the arsonist.
> Bitterness is the trap that snares the hunter.
> And mercy is the choice that can set them all free."
> (Max Lucado "Gods Promises for You").

This is a reason Jesus was sent "... for the opening of the prison to those who are bound." (Isaiah 61:1, NKJV). Forgiveness is the key that unlocks the prison door to set the one that is bound free. Don't be bound by an unforgiving spirit.

~ENJOY YOUR NEW FREEDOM IN CHRIST~

SUMMARY

**We are created to live free!
What then should we remember to do?**

Forgiveness is not an option. You are required to forgive the sins of others or your Father in heaven will not forgive yours.

The Lord said vengeance is His not yours. Give it to God and let go of it as He can do a better job of it. Vengeance is like a poison you are drinking, thinking it will hurt the other person. It doesn't work; it only becomes a raging fire that consumes you.

Keep in mind that the Bible says offenses are constantly coming no matter how nice you are. Your goal is not to become offended.

You are required to forgive everyone including yourself and if you're offended at God, forgive Him also.

Unforgiveness exacts a high price interrupting your prayer life and straining your relationship with God, not to mention the risk of losing God's forgiveness for your sins.
It will wound and steal your peace and joy, leaving you in dire need of healing.

Forgiving a person does not say they were right, or that you even feel like forgiving them, or that God will forgive them. That's between them and God. Forgiving them as an act of your will is for your healing not for theirs.

You simply in prayer say to God "I forgive them as you commanded me to. "Then every time the memory of what they did comes up you say it again and give it to God to delete it from your mind. Eventually the enemy of your soul and your thoughts concerning it will be gone.

~"**Forgiveness is not an occasional act, it is a constant attitude.**"~
Martin Luther King

Scriptures on forgiveness to pray with and find comfort

"Let all bitterness, wrath, anger, clamor, and evil speaking be put away from you, with all malice. And be kind to one another, tenderhearted, forgiving one another, even as God in Christ forgave you."(Ephesians 4:31-32, NKJV).

"Make allowance for each other's faults, and forgive anyone who offends you. Remember, the Lord forgave you, so you must forgive others." (Colossians 3:13, NLT).

"For I can do everything through Christ, who gives me strength." (Philippians 4:13, NLT).

"For with God nothing will be impossible." (Luke 1; 37, NKJV).

"You can ask anything in my name, and I will do it, so that the son can bring glory to the father." (John 14:13, NLT).

"This being so, I myself always strive to have a conscience without offense toward God and men."(Acts 24:16, NKJV).

"All of you, clothe yourselves with humility toward one another, because, "God opposes the proud but shows favor to the humble." (1 Peter 5:5, NIV).

"Therefore let us not judge another anymore, but rather resolve this..." (Romans 14:13, NKJV).

3

Pornography, False Gods, Vain Imaginations And Other Spiders

"You shall have no other gods before Me." (Exodus 20:3, NKJV).
The third of the 10 commandments given from the Most High God states we are to have no other gods and idols in our life.
"For the lord our God is a consuming fire, a jealous God." (Deuteronomy 4:24, NKJV).
"Do nothing out of selfish ambition or vain conceit. Rather, in humility value others above yourselves," (Philippians 2: 3, NIV).

PORNOGRAPHY

The definition of pornography is pictures, films, and writings used only to stimulate sexual desires. It does a lot more than that. I've worked with many men who have been gripped by the spirit of pornea and lust. When it takes hold in a person's life, it rules them like a god. They know they have lost control of their mind and actions at times; but they do not know what to do. I ask them, " It has you, and you don't have it, right?" And they agree. I've had men till me it wakes them up while the family is sleeping and drives them into another room to view the Internet. It's a force they can't seem to stop. For wives, they feel betrayed because their husband is having sex with cyber women. I explain that's it's not their fault as their husband has been dealing with it usually since he was a young teenager long before they met. She is not unable to meet his needs; it's him that cannot control a sinful habit.

Some women view pornography, but it is primarily men because men are attracted by the visual while women are attracted more by what they hear said to them.

The man needs to deal with this as almost all eventually will act out what they are seeing and reacting to. They will email potential sexual partners, escort services, live models, etc. The habit grows and leads to pictures of several women together, groups, masochistic and other stimuli as the old stuff doesn't satisfy them as it once did. Very often the man will ask me if he can get rid of the pictures as they are in his mind all the time— like files that come to the surface. I explain that he can; by capturing every picture and thought, as the Bible says, then asking the Lord to delete it and He will. One must regain control of his body through the power of the Holy Spirit as promised.

"The body is not intended for sexual immorality, but [is intended] for the Lord, and the Lord [is intended] for the body [to save, sanctify and raise it again]. And God both raised the Lord to life and will also raise us up by His power." (1 Corinthians 6: 13-14,Amplified).

Something that I learned that can break this habit as well as others is to encourage the person to start their day proactively by declaring the following

Prayer Strategy:
1.) **I say to my flesh to be in submission to my spirit man. (the spirit is willing but the flesh is weak).**
2.) **Next, say to one's spirit man to be in submission to the Holy Spirit.**
3.) **Then ask the Holy Spirit to crucify the flesh, thereby breaking the habit.**

Saying this daily in a prayer will break it and bring deliverance. Do not believe the lie you can't break it. This has dismantled every spider web of anyone I know that has used it. There is great power when you get lined up spiritually each day.

You will experience the reality that you are not dirty but cleansed by the power of God's blood shed on the cross for you. Watch what you're thinking and cast down every unclean thought. You can do it and you will do it to be free.

I tell the person to quit hiding it and take God into the computer room with them and together He will change their thinking removing it from their mind. Eventually, you will not even want to view it. You renounce this false god and ask the Holy Spirit to crucify your flesh and He will.

God is supreme. He commands us to worship and think only of Him, He does not allow leniency to allow our minds to go anywhere in our thoughts outside of Him- to find a substitute for him. There is to be no fantasy, vain imagination, or lust, to bring release to stress or boredom. We are to find our strength and pleasure in only thoughts of God. The spider, left unchecked, will weave a fantasy world in one's mind to make it easier to find relief from stress or boredom only to ensnare one into a substitute or false god in place of the real one.

"Will they find delight in the Almighty? Will they call on God at all times?" (Job 27:10, NIV).

"Blessed is the one who does not walk in step with the wicked... but whose delight is in the law of the LORD, and who meditates on His law day and night." (Psalms1: 1-2, NIV).

In Ezekiel 38:10,NLT we receive a warning, "This is what the sovereign Lord says: At that time evil thoughts will come to your mind and you will devise a wicked scheme."

In 2 Corinthians 10:5 we are encouraged to capture those rebellious thoughts we have and teach the thoughts to obey Christ.

(See man addicted to pornography in Chapter 5)

"You wonder, am I doomed in my dilemma? I have left the door open for satan, and he has taken advantage of my spiritual passivity. Can I get him out of places he has wormed into?' The answer is a resounding yes! Jesus Christ is the bondage breaker. " (Neil Anderson)

Vain Imaginations

Vain imaginations are always blindness and the Lord knows it.

"...The Lord knoweth the thoughts of the wise, that they are vain." (I Corinthians 3:20, KJV) The word vain 'Mataios' means devoid of truth, useless, fruitless (vanities).

"Let no man deceive you with vain words..." (Ephesians 5: 6,KJV) The 'no man' includes us. We are not to deceive ourselves by telling lies to ourselves. Our flesh within lusted to envy others; we should not pretend to be someone we are not.

"For there shall be no more vain vision nor flattering divination within the house of Israel." (Ezekiel12: 24, KJV).

"For the idols speak delusion; the diviners envision lies, and tell false dreams; they comfort in vain..." (Zechariah10: 2, NKJV).

Seeing visions of one's self that are not true and full of vanity are like what diviners or people do in witchcraft. Some believe evil spirits inject vain imaginations and thoughts into people's minds. I saw a video once that said cults like Scientology actually teach people to imagine themselves as great people from past history. That opens their mind to imagine they are someone they are not.

Consuming Fire

Our God is a consuming fire destroying all thoughts not of Him. Remember, He purifies and cleanses our mind like a computer to be free of viruses. For God consumes us and seeks to destroy any foreign thing. "For the Lord our God is a consuming fire, a jealous God." (Deuteronomy 4: 24,NKJV). "For our God is a consuming fire." (Hebrews 12:12-29,NKJV).

Setup a flytrap
And capture what flies into the mind

Albert Einstein said that people needed to think differently about their issues if they want to solve them. He said "The significant problems we face cannot be solved at the same level of thinking we were on when we created them." We have to change the way we are thinking.

First, ask the Holy Spirit to flag the thoughts that fuel the vain imaginations as you have already decided in your heart it is wrong thinking. Keep a vigilant watch on the dashboard of your mind and keep the trap set.

Then **quarantine (capture)** the thoughts sent often by the enemy that acts as a virus invading the software of your mind. Remember a virus is sent by someone with the intention to harm.

When you intercept the thoughts that come often through the day ask God to delete the thoughts. This frees your mind and brings a continual relief from those obsessive thoughts. Some of the *self-talk* people say to themselves is worse than anything others say to them. It needs to be captured and stopped.

As mentioned before thoughts can invade the mind then **build a stronghold** and distract the person daily sometimes locking them down. A person sometimes cannot concentrate on anything else.

The person can lose control. It becomes a god to the person and it gains control to bring an escape from life's pressures. Instead of going to the Most High for relief, one goes to a dream world of fantasy, to live in.

"The sin in my flesh wars against my mind to bring me into captivity to sin."(See Romans 7:23) Therefore our goal is to capture the thoughts to prevent the mind from being brought into captivity (see 2 Corinthians10: 5).

"Sin wears a cloak of deception. Therefore, the first stage... involves the exposure of our hearts to truth and the cleansing of our hearts from lies...Once the Spirit breaks the power of deception in our lives, He can break the power of sin."
(Francis Frangipane)

This is why Jesus came to fulfill Isaiah 61:1- "to proclaim liberty to the captives, and the opening of the prison to those who are bound."

I have had to be careful about my imaginations. God gives us the ability to use imagination to see into the spirit realm, to imagine what it's like, to understand spiritual concepts and a God we cannot see. But we are not to pretend to be someone of greater importance than we are to feel better about our self.

Vain imaginations set us against the person we are and our destiny planned by God. It is usually fueled by low self-esteem and a lack of active knowledge about who we really are in Christ Jesus. Hurts from the past when we did not perform well encourages us to want to believe other things about ourselves. It can fuel a need to be a different person to live in a fantasy. The truth is we can accept ourselves the way we are, for God loves us just the way we are. He also loves us too much to leave us where we are. In our weakness is when God can pour in His strength to perfect us or bring us to full fruition.

In Christ, we find out who we were always meant to be and then find He actually enables us to grow into it. The life God has planned for us is actually much more exciting than anything we could make up. "Eye has not seen, nor ear heard, nor have entered into the heart of man the things which God has prepared for those who love Him. But God has revealed them to us through His Spirit." (1Corinthians 2: 9-10, NKJV). The Spirit will reveal the wonderful plans God has for each of us.

Vain imaginations will block what God has planned for us. So we must watch what we are thinking and replacing it with truth thus destroying the lies and setting us free to be all God wants us to be!

"Your pain could be God prying open your life and heart to remove a gift of His that you've held on to more dearly than Him" (Tullian Tchividjian). An idol can even be made from something good; but it's an idol if we put it above God. For example, idolizing your ministry above your personal relationship with God.

"Cast your burden on the LORD, and He shall sustain you; He shall never permit the righteous to be moved."(Psalm 55: 22, NKJV). You can do anything in Christ.

Some do not believe they can control their obsessive thoughts but they can. God delights in saving us from all that would seek to destroy us. Remember the **dashboard** and keep monitoring what you're thinking and requesting God to delete the wrong thinking.

"And you, who once were alienated and enemies in your mind by wicked works, yet now He has reconciled in the body of His flesh through death, to present you holy, and blameless and above reproach in His sight—if indeed you continue in the faith, grounded and steadfast, and are not moved away from the hope of the gospel which you heard, which was preached to every creature under heaven, of which I, Paul, became a minister." (Colossians1: 21-23, NKJV).

WE HAVE THE POWER

If you remember, God gave you the ability to control the enemies attacking your mind, and believing that in faith you can then live in the freedom you seek. The reprogramming of the mind is not only possible and doable but also commanded by God. Bring every thought captive and submit it to Him. We have the power to do this or He wouldn't ask it.

We will not find rest when we let our thoughts go astray. "For forty years I was grieved with that generation, and said, 'It is a people who go astray in their hearts, and they do not know My ways.' So I swore in My wrath, they shall not enter My rest." (Psalm 95: 10-11,NKJV).

When we reconcile our thoughts to God, we can cease striving and enter a peaceful rest with our minds stayed on the One who is our Savior. When we are worried and anxiety-ridden, we are letting fear be triumphant over our faith in Jesus.

CASTING DOWN ARGUMENTS

We have talked a lot about capturing our negative untrue thoughts and deleting them.

We need to emphasize when the thoughts become arguments then we've accepted them; and actually are expending our own energy protecting them. We try to keep them secret allowing the enemy to hide. We actually guarantee him access to our mind. We must see these hiding places, expose them, and work on undoing the argument that keeps them.

"The weapons we fight with are not the weapons of the world. On the contrary, they have divine power to demolish strongholds. We demolish arguments and every pretension that sets itself up against the knowledge of God, and we take captive every thought to make it obedient to Christ." (2 Cor. 10:4-5,NIV)

For example anger, for some, can be like an old friend. They don't want to lose it because it gets them up to do things they don't want to do. It defends them from other people that threaten them etc., when it may be a constant negative emotion because the person lives in fear or is obsessed with control.

We must cast down or demolish arguments that are holding us back-we are commanded to. Remember you are armed to fight the battle.

The effective weapon to free us is to find and take apart false arguments that gets us to believe that which is against the knowledge of God. How do we see these arguments that we have always believed but are untrue?

"I keep asking that the God of our Lord Jesus Christ, the glorious Father, may give you the Spirit of wisdom and revelation, so that you may know Him better.

I pray that the eyes of your heart may be enlightened in order that you may know the hope to which He has called you, the riches of His glorious inheritance in his holy people, and his incomparably great power for us who believe." (Ephesians 1: 17-19, NIV).

To gain wisdom and revelation to see and understand spiritual things that comes from the Holy Spirit working with us through the eyes of our heart. The eyes of our heart being our mind. So our mind sees and understands with the help of the Holy Spirit.

The Holy Spirit leads and guides us in truth. That truth separates the arguments we've believed that are not true. For example, a person says I cannot lose weight. How do they know that because they have tried and have not been able to do it? The argument that they cannot lose weight has been won, and so they are slowly dying of diabetes, high cholesterol and heart trouble because of the heavy weight. The truth is that they can do anything through the power of God. They have learned they can't, but the false argument can be unlearned with the help of the Holy Spirit. A new argument is then learned that they can do all things. They pray about it and the Holy Spirit teaches them to depend on Him when they are nervous and want to over eat. They suddenly feel led to channel their nervous energy into exercise and loosing weight with a new discipline they've never had before. God worked it all together for good because they prayed and the Holy Spirit led them to see a new truth through the eyes of their heart. He then strengthened them to overcome.

Jesus Christ must be our only God we trust in. "The mature Christians I have met along the way are those who have failed and have learned to live gracefully with their failure. Faithfulness requires the courage to risk everything on Jesus, the willingness to keep growing, and the readiness to risk failure throughout our lives." ("The Ragamuffin Gospel " by Brennan Manning).

~A GOOD PRAYER~

"**May I grow more sure of Thy reality and power: May I attain a clearer mind as to the meaning of my life on earth: May I strengthen my hold upon life eternal: May I look more and more to the things unseen: May my desires grow less unruly and my imaginations more pure:**"("**A Diary of Private Prayer" by John Baillie).**

4

THE NEED FOR SAFE BOUNDARIES FROM ANY WEB

> *"...but we walk in deep shadows. Like the blind we grope along the wall, feeling our way like people without eyes."(Isaiah 59:9-10,NIV) We will need God's eyes to see where we need to set our walls or boundaries in our relationships, in order to move from darkness to light.*

God has ordained that we are to be in relationships and work together in the body to move forward the kingdom of heaven. The Lord said faith and hope are good things to accomplish but love is the greatest. We can do lots of ministry but if it is without love, It's just a lot of noise. Love is greatest because it requires the most unselfishness and work to accomplish. If I have learned anything about love, it was watching how God loves me. He is so forgiving and caring of me as a person.

Since we are meant to have good healthy relationships, the spider works to disrupt, pervert, and even destroy relationships we have. Therefore the spider webs he likes to use revolve around improper boundaries with other people. Some people have no boundaries, and others have improper ones. This can all be corrected when one knows what the boundaries should be to bring needed liberty.

LIBERTY VS FREEDOM

None of us have complete freedom to do whatever we want. We don't live in a free country. People aren't free to take my car because they see and like it better than theirs.

We do have liberty that is freedom to work within certain boundaries. I am free to go out and buy a car, but not steal one. In a relationship a young single lady has the right to have a boundary of abstinence. A young single man is breaking that boundary if he tries to get her to have sex with him. It's because boundaries are either broken or not set that abuse and breach of a person's freedom occurs. You've heard the expression "He's taking liberties he doesn't have."

Boundaries keep people safe and allow a relationship to grow and flourish. There can be a lack of boundaries in marriage, family, work and friendships of all kinds. Even God has boundaries in his relationship with us. In the very beginning Adam and Eve were told what they could and could not do. They broke the boundary God set and He then moved them out of the Garden and set a boundary with an angel to enforce it so they could not come back in. We used an example earlier in this book that you may have to call the police if a neighbor doesn't respect your property boundaries and is attempting to steal from you. There may be things you need the police to do to establish proper boundaries that will make your life with others much better.

"The fear of man brings a snare, but whoever trusts in the Lord shall be safe." (Proverbs 29:25, NCV). We are not to fear what others think only God.

There was a mother who gave her son whatever he wanted. Later when he was older, he demanded money and stole from her if she didn't give it. She had to eventually place him in foster care because he did not respect her boundaries. How did this happen? How was the web spun that created this crisis? In her mind she felt bad because the son lost his father due to a divorce. The guilt she felt led her to give him whatever he wanted. That's not love that's guilt. God does not give us everything we want. He is quite capable, thank goodness, of saying no so we do not become a taker but learn to be a giver.

In this case the mother cared for her son but false guilt kept her from seeing the truth. Setting a boundary for her son early in his life would have freed him from stealing and abusing his mother. He didn't have a father because the father did not want to be in the marriage or in his son's life. She was accepting guilt for a situation not of her making. She needed to release the guilt of the past and raise her son as God intended—to teach him proper boundaries of right and wrong.

WE MUST HAVE BOUNDARIES to keep the spider out

A wife allowed her husband to batter her because she was taught that was permissible Biblically since he was the head of the household. The spider spun a web that a husband can do improper things like physically hurt her since he was the head of the household. The Bible teaches the truth that the husband is head of the household as Christ is head of the church who laid down his life for His bride the church. The Bible doesn't teach the wife to do whatever the husband says if he asks her to submit and do ungodly things. If he asks her to rob a bank would she be required to do it? No. She should not do or accept any ungodly behavior whether it's from a husband or a pastor or anyone. The husband is to lay down his life and protect her not beat her. For her safety she needs to set a boundary against the husbands abuse releasing that lie and living the truth. The truth is she has the right to be safe, and just as she sets a boundary against anyone hurting her on the street; the same goes for her husband. He has no mandate to ask her to do or accept ungodly things.

You can begin to see by these two examples how powerful proper boundaries can be.

They can literally change people's lives. Boundaries define not only what I do but also who I am. As a child of God I should expect not to live under tyranny and lies but to live in freedom under Christ Jesus.

The first thing a person needs to do is give themselves permission to say "NO". That may sound simple but it isn't. To say no is to set a boundary. To say no you will have to have a valid reason so you will enforce it. That reason should come from God and or His Word. For example, it's wrong if a wife says the husband does not love her if he doesn't allow her to spend money they cannot pay back.

The opposite is true He doesn't love her and the family if he approves of ungodly spending. The Bible makes it clear **"...The borrower is servant to the lender." (Proverbs 22:7, Amplified).**

That's idolatry when someone trusts in debt to buy things instead of trusting God for their needs. When you know that God says no and does not give you permission you will be better able to tell yourself or someone else no.

If you have a boss that constantly asks you to work overtime because others he asks says no; then you know what you must do for yours and your family's sake.

You know that because God expects you not to make work your God. You will be able to say no to the boss in order to please God. If you will put God first he promised he would add everything else unto you. You will not have to fear losing your job because God will replace it with a better one, if He is put first in your life.

When a false reason for doing something comes up and you overcome it in Christ, you will grow significantly. If you cannot say no people will take advantage of you, remember this: - **when you are saying yes to someone, then remember you are also saying no to everyone else including yourself.** You are not growing and God created you to keep advancing and overcoming. Servers, those who serve because they do not want to disappoint anyone are ones who desperately need to understand that truth. If a father says yes to a client who wants to meet after office hours, then he must remember his family obligations; his child's ball game and his wife's need for help at home, or he has then said 'no' to them. Who are you going to say yes to determines whom you say no to? If he honors God his family and himself then God will take care of what his client thinks.

EVERYONE CAN LEARN HOW TO SAY NO

A good rule to follow, when dealing with tough but needed boundaries in relationships, is to confront the brutal facts with hope. You break the stronghold by admitting what you're doing isn't working. Then confront it, and with God's help finding hope as He leads you to the answer.

The freedom people will receive by learning how to say no and setting boundaries is incredible. May I encourage you to start small with little no's and then no to more important things. When you know you will be disappointing God if you don't say no to people then it will become easier and easier.

Self-control is a fruit of the Spirit (see Galatians 5:22&23). We must repair the walls that have crumbled in our life. Ask the Holy Spirit to help you read those thoughts on your **dashboard** you need to change to make repairs on your walls.

"Like a city whose walls are broken through is a person who lacks self-control." (Proverbs 25:28, NIV). Without set boundaries we become like a city being invaded because we have let our walls break down.

There are many books on the subject of boundaries that explore this subject to a much greater degree. The purpose of this book is to give brief, practical, biblically- based information to break spider webs and remove the spider that is using lies to keep you bound.

Before we leave this subject, remember the biblical truth that we reap what we sow. That is, if you do not change what you're doing in your relationships, then you will continue reaping poor relationships. If you will sow into your relationships the truth that you have permission to say no, then you will reap tremendous freedom to better please God. You will be saying yes to God and no to man when it's appropriate. It is sinful to not say yes to God in every area of our life. God, of course, ask us to obey because he has a freer and flourishing life for us to enjoy.

"We change our behavior when the pain of staying the same becomes greater than the pain of changing. Consequences give us the pain that motivates us to change." (Henry Cloud)

~**"Do not be deceived: God cannot be mocked. A man reaps what he sows. Whoever sows to please their flesh, from the flesh will reap destruction; whoever sows to please the Spirit, from the Spirit will reap eternal life."(Galatians 6:7-8, NIV).** ~

SUMMARY

**We are created to live free!
What then should we remember to do?**

Boundaries keep us safe and we must remember when we say yes to one thing we are saying no to another.

Even God set boundaries with Adam and Eve.

We are to have personal boundaries that God has designed for us as He has shared in His Word.

You will know when to say yes when you bring it before God and are seeking to please Him only. When you put Him first, He will reconcile people unto you.

He will guide you and keep you safe. You only have to then obey and set your needed boundary for a given relationship.

God has made it clear that the only one you have to please is Him. If you do that According to the Word then He will add everything unto to you.

"Guard your heart above all else, for it determines the course of your life." (Proverbs 4:23, NLT).

SCRIPTURES TO MEDITATE

"Those who spare the rod of discipline hate their children. Those who love their children care enough to discipline them." (Proverbs 13:24, NLT).

"Whoever abandons the right path will be severely disciplined; whoever hates correction will die."(Proverbs 15:10, NLT).

"Train up a child in the way he should go: and when he is old, he will not depart from it." (Proverbs 22: 6, KJV).

"So the Lord God banished him from the Garden of Eden to work the ground from which he had been taken" (Genesis 3:23, NIV).

"The name of the LORD [is] a strong tower: the righteous runneth into it, and is safe." (Proverbs 18:10, KJV).

"Be ye not unequally yoked together with unbelievers: for what fellowship hath righteousness with unrighteousness? And what communion hath light with darkness." (2 Corinthians 6:14, KJV).

"Keep me from the snares they have laid for me, and from the traps of the workers of iniquity, let the wicked fall into their own nets, while I escape safely."(Psalm 141:9-10, NKJV)

5

INNER HEALING AND DELIVERANCE FROM THE SPIDER

"...uttering lies our hearts have conceived." "...Truth has stumbled in the streets, honesty cannot enter. Truth is nowhere to be found." (Isaiah 59:13-15, NIV). When we replace the lies, we've come to believe with the truth. Then we heal.

Christians are struggling with sins having lost all hope through a series of thoughts that have convinced them in their mind to give up. Things like men on pornography, ladies on habit forming prescription drugs, teenagers with eating disorders etc.. But Christ came to set people free who are held captive.

When one receives their salvation and the forgiveness of their sins, then they can see better. The blindfold of the enemy is removed. "For the god of this world [satan] has blinded the unbelievers' minds [that they should not discern the truth], preventing them from seeing the illuminating light of the Gospel of the glory of Christ, (the Messiah)."(2 Corinthians 4:4, Amplified).

People come in to see me who are embarrassed that they have a besetting sin in their life they haven't been able to overcome. Other people have told them to just get saved; but they are saved. People have told them they need the power of the Holy Spirit, but they are filled with the Spirit.

WE ARE NOT TO LIVE WITH GUILT

Guilt ridden, feeling defeated and disappointed in themselves, they blame themselves. They are right where the enemy wants them especially when they are so embarrassed to mention their failures that they hide them. When the enemy the spider can isolate them in their sin, then he can hold them in his web. He can then literally suck the life out of them. Hiding their sin and turning away from the church for help often results in anger being turned inward (depression). Also their anger is turned against God. After all, where is He?

Beware of the spider

You see, the strategy of the spider is to isolate. Through a series of false arguments he successfully has cut them off from help, especially the only sources of help that could defeat the spider. Even better is when they are not aware of the spider that has spun the web of lies in their mind. Then they are only looking at their own inability to break free and not the one dedicated to rob, steal, and destroy them.

I have come to believe the Spider has two goals. One goal is to get the person once saved, to turn away from God. If that's not possible, then he gets them to feel they are not good enough to serve God and therefore he paralyzes them spiritually so they can't hurt him.

This is the state of many people going to church. They're not serving as they feel they are not worthy enough because of their sins. The requirement to serve is not being sinless but forgiven. God's Word says, I will "console those who mourn in Zion,"

(Isaiah 61:3, NKJV). Zion is a word also used for Jerusalem or in other translations saying Israel referring to God's people. God will come along side of His people and comfort them. "To grant [consolation and joy] to those who mourn in Zion, to give them an ornament -a garland or diadem-of beauty instead of ashes, the oil of joy for mourning, the garment [expressive] of praise instead of a heavy, burdened and failing spirit;..." (Isaiah 61: 3, Amplified).

The Bible says that all have sinned and fallen short of the glory of God. No one but Jesus can walk in perfection. But through a series of arguments in their mind, they believe they must walk in victory because they know what is the right thing to do is. Just because they know what to do does not mean they know how. They do need to take the first step to admit they are having a problem and are in trouble.

I tell people if you are willing to endure a little pain now then it's possible you could receive a healing that will last forever.

A crisis can be a good motivator to work on the disciplines needed in the mind. Without a crisis, many lack motivation to do the work. The pain from the past otherwise could last for one's lifetime.

Oswald Chambers said, "The discipline of our mind is the one domain God has put in our keeping." While it is under our control, we have to choose to discipline our thinking in order to operate in truth.

I have found there are usually only 2-3 strands undergirding the spider's web. When those are dealt with the web falls apart. The Holy Spirit can identify those strands by uncovering the original lies like I'm rejected, unclean, unworthy, trapped and can't get out etc. Those foundational lies were usually established in childhood. Once uncovered and replaced with the truth the web falls apart. It's remarkable how powerful the web was and how free the person can be for the first time in their life.

For example, there was a teenager who was bulimic and nearly died from the disorder.

It turned out that it had started several years before when another school friend had said they thought the person was gaining weight. Then a series of arguments came into her mind. That fat was evil and the opposite sex would not like them and other kids would criticize their appearance. Food was then evil because it led to being fat. The truth is that God made food for our nourishment, but she started to believe the lie.

"And God said, See, I have given you every plant yielding seed that is on the face of all the land, and every tree with seed in its fruit; you shall have them for food." (Genesis 1: 29, Amplified).

Fat is evil so food must be evil to. Therefore she must purge the food that was evil to keep from being fat that was evil. She felt guilty doing this, would eat again; but would have to purge it, then feeling guilty again. It was a cycle spun by the spider that was killing her.

Having seen the lies, I took her to scripture in Genesis where it said food was created for our nourishment and was not evil. In fact we will eat food in heaven.

Then fat was not evil as all of us have a certain measure of body fat meant to keep us warm, etc. Even full-bodied women in the Renaissance Period where considered the most beautiful, not pencil thin bodies that are valued today.

We discussed that it was probably not a good idea to let other people's comments have that much control over us. We prayed a prayer renouncing the lies and declaring the truth that food was not evil and neither was fat.

She left the office and never came back. The power of the lies was broken by the truth. A lie can be as powerful as the truth if you believe it; this lie was refuted.

AS MENTIONED WE OFTEN DO NOT LIVE WITH THE FACTS BUT WITH THE STORY WE TELL OURSELVES ABOUT WHAT HAPPENED.

This has always been a marvel to me that the mind could be convinced of a lie and how that lie could destroy or kill a person. A person comes out of the womb fighting for its first breath with an innate survivor mentality. This is a God given mentality to do what ever is necessary to live. Yet through a series of arguments in the mind, it can be replaced with a mindset actually convincing the person to kill himself or herself. A person on their own doesn't do that; it's unnatural as well as ungodly. It's the power of deception that the enemy has learned to use very effectively

"They conceive trouble and give birth to evil; their womb fashions deceit. " (Job15: 35, NIV). The idea comes through that it is not true; but it is allowed to conceive and give birth to evil. One of the great tools of the spider is discouragement. When we are discouraged we don't even try to break free. Our will is broken. "There is no possibility for discouragement if we will only remember that this is the relationship, not God's blessing, but Himself." (Oswald Chambers). In other words what does it matter what is coming against us if we will only remember that He whom we are in relationship with is the most powerful one in the universe. He is the source of our encouragement.

There was a man with an addiction to pornography. It led to chat rooms and then to emailing women he wasn't married to. A man is what he thinks; and therefore what he's thinking will lead to his acting it out. He had been looking at pornography since he was a child as his father had it in the house. He was about to lose his wife and family because of the actions brought about by this addiction.

"For as he thinks in his heart, so is he." (Proverbs 23:7, Amplified).

We asked the Holy Spirit to help take him to the place in his childhood that was significant. The spider may have many layers to his web but as already mentioned only two or three main strands usually hold them in place.

Just like spider webs in a barn or in a bush if you cut the main strands the whole spider web falls down. The Holy Spirit knows where the two or three memories are that structured the lies of the stronghold and if one finds and destroys them, then like an Achilles heel, the spider's web is disabled. If people only knew that only a few past experiences are holding them back from the wonderful future they could have in Christ.

UNDOING SPIDER WEBS BY UNDOING THE FEW MAIN STRANDS

When he went into prayer we simply asked for the Holy Spirit to reveal which memories are important. We do not need to know everything that has happened in the past only what the Holy Spirit brings to mind when we ask him. There were several memories that came to his mind and they were ones he has seen at other times. I believe the Holy Spirit tries to tell the person where they need to go to find the lies they are living with. We go to that memory and the person discovers what he is thinking at the time. That's all we need to know not all the details. He was thinking that intimacy and deeper friendship were not necessary to satisfy ones self sexually. Also, that sex was more of something he could use to release tension and satisfy a curiosity of doing something he was not suppose to when his parents were not in the house.

We discussed that it's a lie that sex is more gratifying and easier with pictures of people he has no emotional attachment. It does not satisfy as he has found out. He found out what others have found out in similar situations, he has to enhance the pictures. They may start with unclothed people but graduate to many other pictures of sexual acts and eventually live models. It never satisfies fully and escalates into even more sinful activity.

It's sinful in that he is having sex with other women whether he is physically with them or not. If he just lusted after other women the bible teaches he is committing adultery. "But I say to you that whoever looks at a woman to lust for her has already committed adultery with her in his heart." (Matthew 5:28, NKJV).

Because he is going to pornography to quickly release tension, instead of prayer with God-he is committing Idolatry. He is not turning to God but something else to receive a release from his craving instead of solving the problem. Once he admitted the lies and asked forgiveness for the sins committed —the strands were broken and the web caved in. The spider of pornea and lust were cast out and the man was free. He then began having fulfilling sex with his wife and was delivered by God.

Another person was molested by a relative for a number of years. They were told as a child that while it was normal they must keep it a secret. We discussed that an adult having sex with a minor was wrong even in the secular world. That they were a victim not the perpetrator of that sinful behavior. They no longer needed to live as a victim. Their life would no longer be defined by what someone did to them but by Christ who died for them. She was pure and clean having been cleansed by God forever. She let the secret out and was finally free of any false guilt.

Establish a No-Spin Zone
Train your mind not to allow lies to be spun into webs by watching your **dashboard**.

People who have been sexually violated need to know that it is not what comes into a person's body that defiles them; but what comes out of their heart. "For from within, out of the heart of men, proceeds evil thoughts adulteries, fornications, murders, thefts, covetousness, wickedness, deceit, lewdness, an evil eye, blasphemy, pride, foolishness. All these evil things come from within and defile a man."(Mark 7:21-23, NKJV). It was not what physically came into the person that defiled a person. It is what comes out of their heart. When they confessed the truth and renounced the lies of the web that had held them so long, then it's broken. The spider of low self-esteem, and a poor self-image was removed. The person no longer let others abuse them because they were no longer a victim. She could say no to people who would abuse her and hurt her because she knew now that she was of great value as Christ died for her. She found a new self-esteem in the one who had died for her.

DELIVERED FROM THE KINGDOM OF DARKNESS

Their life was changed from a victim mentality to more than a conqueror in Christ.

"For sin shall not have dominion over you, for you are not under the law but under grace." (Romans 6: 14, NKJV) People don't believe they can be free because there is besetting sin that they have tried to break to no avail. They have prayed, ask others to pray, they have read and claimed the word yet it's still there. That experience has built a web of lies that this sin will have dominion over them. They do not know why but they can't break it.

The spider not only wrapped them in the web but also has disabled their will to even try and break it.

They are convinced in their mind that it's a lost cause even though the Word says ALL sin shall not have dominion over you.

What does one do? They start claiming what the Bible says believing the Author can be trusted. The web can be undone the same way it was built by finding the foundational thoughts it was built on as in the examples above. We must pick up and use the spiritual weapons we've been learning are available to us.

"For the weapons of our warfare are not carnal but mighty in God for pulling down strongholds, casting down arguments and every high thing that exalts itself against the knowledge of God, bringing every thought into captivity to the obedience of Christ, and being ready to punish all disobedience when your obedience is fulfilled."(2 Corinthians 10:4-6, NKJV).

Trap The Spider

To trap the spider It's important to be honest about what you're dealing with before the Lord. The spider then becomes exposed through honesty. God's not embarrassed and so neither should you. The spider is terrified of the humble soul surrendered to God. He wants you to hide your sin and not let it out in the sunlight where you could be healed.

"Then you will know the truth and the truth will set you free" (John 8:32,NIV).

Keep choosing to live in a No-Spin Zone

Continue training your mind to identify and capture lies you keep thinking.

The sinful habits actually give the spider a place to hide-don't let him. Repenting of sinful thoughts and actions actually enables the deliverance and can lead to many other healings. When your thoughts agree with the sin the enemy is more secure. You will find the strength of the sin when you attempt to break it. The spider's stronghold is just a web spun with lies and he has made a house of thoughts. The real truth will cast him and his lies out.

As we have described above, ask the Holy Spirit to reveal the lies that created them casting them out and refusing to believe them as truth. This is the way you fight to overturn your enemies by undoing their evil arguments with what is right according to the Bible.

When overcoming the flesh remember the **Prayer Strategy**. Every morning when one gets up align yourself under God by saying" I say to my flesh be in submission to my spirit man; and my spirit man to be in submission to the Holy Spirit. (The spirit man is willing to do the right thing but the flesh is too weak.) Then ask for the Holy Spirit's help whose job it is to crucify the flesh. He will always do it if you ask. He can conquer any addiction or problem and give you the victory. You are commanded not to let sin reign even if you are willing to live with it.

"therefore do not let sin reign in your mortal body, that you should obey it in its lusts." (Romans 6:12, NKJV).

"Therefore, brothers, we have an obligation-but it is not to the sinful nature, to live according to it. For if you live according to the sinful nature, you will die; but if by the Spirit you put to death the misdeeds of the body, you will live." (Romans 8:12-13, NIV).

"So If the Son sets you free, you will be free indeed." (John 8:36, NIV).

TRANSFORMED LITTLE BY LITTLE

You got saved from your sin when you accepted Christ but for the rest of your life little by little you will be saved from your old nature that is your old way of thinking. Don't worry this is not done in your strength because if you were strong enough you would have already done it. The Holy Spirit who is stronger than you will bring your flesh under control. Like the Israelites taking the Promised Land little by little so you will conquer the obligations you lived under by your old man and start living in a new freedom under the power of the Holy Spirit.

The Holy Spirit is able to crucify your flesh. Live broken and crucified in order to have more of Christ in control. The more yielded we are to Christ the more control we actually gain.

Along with the **Prayer Strategy** you may also put on each piece of the spiritual armor in prayer every morning when you arise. You simply speak it in prayer: Holy Spirit I ask you to put on me the helmet of salvation, the breastplate of righteousness, the belt of truth, the shoes of peace and the shield of faith and the sword of the spirit and to pray always.

The above prayers said in faith taking only minutes to say but they will enable you with the Holy Spirit's help to overcome both the flesh and the enemy.

"... in all these things we are more than conquerors through him who loved us." (Romans 8:37, NIV). **"More"** meaning we will not only conquer but come out stronger not weaker, having battled for our new freedom in Christ.

We become like Paul who said "For I am convinced that neither death nor life, neither angels nor demons, neither the present nor the future, nor any powers, neither height nor depth, nor anything else in all of creation, will be able to separate us from the love of God that is in Christ Jesus our Lord." (Romans 8:38-39, NIV). That pretty well covers it all. In Christ nothing can stop us until we get the victory doing it in His strength not our own.

While in battle or at anytime I am discouraged, I have learned I can ask God for encouragement and He will always bring it. Try it as it will help you persevere and stay in the fight until you win.

DELIVERANCE FROM THE SPIDER (THE ENEMY)

I'm convinced the enemy of our soul uses two defenses: One is denial that you do not have a problem so you do not deal with it. The second is you may have a problem but you will not bring it up and work on it as it will cause you too much pain.

If a person can get past these two defenses then they are on a pathway to healing. The enemy knows if one brings out the secret sin into the sunlight they might get healed. He wants to keep them ashamed so they will hide their sinful behaviors. The spider builds his web of lies as a strongman constructing a house with gates or doors and he can go in and out of to repair any breaches. The house is the mind of the one he holds captive.

"Who is powerful enough to enter the house of a strong man like satan and plunder his goods? Only someone even stronger—someone who could tie him up and then plunder his house." (Mark 3:27, NLT). You have the Holy Spirit who guides you in truth who can tie up the spider who is spinning the webs in your mind that controls you. It's His truth that sets you free untying all things that have bound you. The Lord promises to contend with those who contend with us. (See Isaiah 49:25, NIV).

We find the doors to the house of the spider with the help of the Holy Spirit who shows us in prayer. Also He helps us scrutinize our thoughts and what we are thinking. Then we use the divine weapons of God mentioned earlier (2 Corithians10:4). Bring captive every thought that seeks to build a house of lies that is against the knowledge God and your freedom. Then keep the thoughts out by dismissing them when they come to mind. The door is shut and the spider has lost his access to your mind in that area. With his access denied he should be bound and permanently removed.

Bind and cast out the spider

We then ask the Holy Spirit to bind him and remove him sending him into the hands of Jesus never to return. Remember your words spoken in prayer are powerful. We close the door he was using by declaring truth instead of the lies. Jesus refers to these gates or doors "...I will build My church (God's house), and the gates of Hades shall not prevail against it. And I will give you the keys of the Kingdom of heaven, and whatever you bind on earth will be bound in heaven, and whatever you loose on earth will be loosed in heaven." (Matthew 16:18-19, NKJV)

A key represents authority. The one who is entrusted with a key to something has the authority to open the door and gain access. Whatever door or gate the enemy is using defensibly to guard his spider web can be opened with the master key.

You can then remove the gates of the enemy with access to the house he occupied in your mind and remove his evil goods. Then you have the authority to bind him and remove him in Christ's name who has defeated him. When I was knocking down spider webs around the outside of my house I found they were back up the next day. I learned after tearing down a spider web you have to also remove the spider permanently.

After breaking down what the spider had built, it's important to remove the spider using the keys to the Kingdom of God he has given us. Bind the spider, the enemy of Christ, and send them into the hands of Jesus Christ.

Then your deliverance can be completed.

I learned from Derek Prince that by asking God to cut off and remove any curses and familiar spirits that may have been passed down from our birth mother and father can very often bring a new freedom to succeed. Also in prayer, claim all the blessings God gave Abraham to prosper in every way: physically, spiritually, mentally, and emotionally.

I believe God showed me the counterfeit armor the enemy uses that must be taken off and replaced with His Godly armor by the Holy Spirit.

Spiritual Armor	Enemy	Holy Spirit
Helmet of Salvation	Blinds the mind	protects the Mind
Breastplate of Righteousness	Feeling unworthy	Christ righteousness
Belt of Truth	Lies	Truth
Shoes of peace	Worry/Anxiety	Supernatural Peace
Shield of Faith	Doubt/Fear	Faith/trust
Sword of the Spirit	Deception	Word of God
Pray Always	constantly defending	Talking to God

The helmet of salvation protects our mind and reminds us that though we have faults we are forgiven and saved from those faults.

Though we fail we are righteous in Christ Jesus and made worthy as we have access to the real, not imagined truth. If we forgive others, we walk in a peace that is supernatural. We not only have faith but also trust that God will help us overcome fear and doubt. I can rest in the Lord no longer needing to keep defending myself.

Take the enemy's armor off and put on God's armor
When one successfully removes the enemy's blindfolds as discussed then one can see. If one is feeling unworthy they are not accepting the robes of Jesus righteousness. When deception is overcome in truth it's the beginning of freedom. When consumed with worry and anxiety then you know you are not trusting in God's promises that overcome those feelings. Fear must be removed or the person lives in torment. When one knows the Word of God then they can know the difference between what is a lie or not. In constantly defending yourself, one does not believe you're free of the past and what other people think. You are secure when you stay in contact with the Lord daily.

"For he has rescued us from the dominion of darkness and brought us into the kingdom of the Son he loves, in whom we have redemption, the forgiveness of sins." (Colossians 1:13-14, NIV).

We are safe in this world in Christ Jesus.
The enemy is a strongman who holds you captive in place by his armor built on untruths. When you undo those untruths with the truth then you disarm the strongman. "But when a stronger than he comes upon him and overcomes him, he takes from him all his armor in which he trusted, and divides his spoils." (Luke11: 22, NKJV). When you remove his armor he has held you captive with then the spoils of that victory is a self that is now unbound. It is Jesus who is stronger than your adversary and the one who can disarm him when you ask. "Having disarmed principalities and powers, he made a public spectacle of them, triumphing over them in it." (Colossians2: 15 NKJV).

"Dear Jesus, if I get a red wagon for Christmas, I will eat all my vegetables for a year." Then Johnnie thought, *Oh, no, that means spinach, broccoli and asparagus. Yuck! I could never ever keep that promise.*

Suddenly Johnnie had an idea. He went downstairs to the living room. From the mantel above the fireplace, he grabbed the family's statue of the Virgin Mary. Taking the statue to the kitchen he wrapped it in newspapers and stuffed it into a grocery bag. He took the bag upstairs to his room, opened the closet and placed the package in the farthest, darkest corner.

He then closed the closet door, took a new sheet of paper and wrote, "Dear Jesus, if you ever want to see your mother again..."

~Just like the little boy, satan tries to make you believe he has something he really doesn't have and power he does not possess. ~

SUMMARY

We are created to live free!
What then should we remember to do?

Use God's weapons capturing thoughts and finding any lies replacing them with the truth. Watch our self-talk and compare it to the truth found in the Word. If we are saying we cannot control ourselves the Bible says we can do all things through Christ who strengthens me.

When a memory keeps coming back, then ask the Holy Spirit why. He may be directing you to the original lie you started believing. We often do not live with the facts, but the lies we have told ourselves.

The enemy tells us lies in the hope we will believe it in order to control us. He builds his cobwebs with his deception to hold us.

When we discover the lie, we only have to renounce it in prayer with the Lord.
Then replace it with truth from the Word. Then the web is broken and we are free.

Remove the enemy's spiritual armor which blinds our minds with lies, telling us we are unworthy, deceiving us, bringing worry, fears and constantly defending ourselves. Put on God's spiritual armor protecting our salvation putting on Christ's righteousness, with peace, faith, the Word, and always talking to God.

Scriptures to meditate

"A good man's mind is filled with honest thoughts; and evil man's mind is crammed with lies." (Proverbs 12:5, The Living bible).

"A good man is known by truthfulness a false man by deceit and lies." (Proverbs 12:17, The Living Bible).

"And you shall know the truth, and the truth shall make you free." (John 8:32, NKJV).

"Therefore submit to God. Resist the devil and he will flee from you. Draw near to God and He will draw near to you." (James 4:7, NKJV).

"But thanks be to God, who gives us the victory through our Lord Jesus Christ." (1 Corinthians 15: 57, NKJV).

"For by wise counsel thou shalt make thy war: and in multitude of counselors [there is] safety." (Proverbs 24:6, KJV).

"I, I am the One who forgives all your sins, for my sake; I will not remember your sins." (Isaiah 43:25, NCV).

"I leave you peace; my peace I give you. I do not give it to you as the world does. So don't let your hearts be troubled or afraid." (John 14:27, NCV).

"LORD, even when I have trouble all around me, you will keep me alive. When my enemies are angry, you will reach down and save me by your power." (Psalm 138:7, NCV).

6

Sustaining Freedom After Being Delivered From The Spider.

"And He saw that there was no man, and wondered that there was no intercessor [no one to intervene on behalf of truth and right]; therefore His own arm brought Him victory, and his righteousness [having the Spirit without measure] sustained Him." (Isaiah 59:16, Amplified)

One must intercede and believe the Messiah can bring salvation every day and sustain you. Then call on Him and His truth to maintain the freedom from spiders and the cobwebs of lies.

Intercession is the key to keeping your victory in Christ. One must keep his relationship with God strong and intimate to withstand the constant assaults of the enemy trying to destroy him. Cling to God who is the one who can deliver you. It's cultivating a love relationship with God that gives one strength and peace while the fight goes on.

"For thus said the Lord God, the Holy One of Israel, In returning to Me and resting in Me you shall be saved; in quietness and in (trusting) confidence shall be your strength. And you would not." (Isaiah 30:15, Amplified)
Make sure you are not the one who fails to return to God for their daily needs of salvation. He is our hope and our salvation each day.

Do not fear that the enemy has won and you never will. That he is too strong and you are too weak. Your strength and your victory does not depend on yourself but with the mighty God of all the ages. He will defend and deliver you in His own strength and you can put your faith in that.
There is a story about George Washington in the battle of Monongahela whereby He had 2 horses shot out from underneath him. The Indian sharpshooters were told to target him; but couldn't kill him. Even though they killed every other officer on horseback in fact only 30 soldiers lived. An Indian named Redhawk predicted that Washington would never die in battle and be the founder of a mighty empire. The Indians surmised that Washington was under a special guardianship of the Great Spirit.

We are under the guardianship of the great and mighty God of all the ages and we will not die but live in victory.
You see being one with God allows us to rest knowing we have the victory through the power of the Most High. The amazing thing is that this relationship is not only allowed but requested by the Son of God.

"So that they all may be one [just] as You, Father, are in Me and I in You, that they may also be one in Us, so that the world may believe and be convinced that You have sent Me." (John 17:21, Amplified).

This is incredible that we in our spirit man can be joined as one with the Father and Son of God just as they are. It means that no matter what the situation is we are unified with God and He therefore can work all things together for our good. "Depend on the LORD; Trust him and he will take care of you," (Psalm 37:5, NCV).

Being joined with God in a relationship allows us to constantly have access to the truth since He is the Truth. He will instruct us in the truth that we might understand and not be held captive by the enemy who is the father of lies and has so easily ensnared us.

> "Gently instruct those who oppose the truth. Perhaps God will change those people's hearts, and they will learn the truth. Then they will come to their senses and escape from the devils trap. For they have been held captive by him to do whatever he wants."(2 Timothy 2:25-26, NLT).

The enemy lies, but we still believe it somehow, like this joke below by Ben Bailey.
"I have a friend. He keeps trying to convince me he's a compulsive liar, but I don't believe him."

You see the need to stay close to God, walking with Him that He might protect you from the one who battles for your mind, to bring false arguments for you to believe that sets you against the knowledge of God. Lies and sin of the flesh separate us from God.

Our flesh, as we have found out, will actually rule our lives and lead to a spiritual death rather than to spiritual life renewed daily by the power of God. We must put to death our old man, or flesh, and crucify him so we may walk in freedom.
Paul said, "But I discern in my bodily members-in the sensitive appetites and wills of the flesh-a different law (rule of action) at war against the law of my mind (my reason) and making me a prisoner to the law of sin that dwells in my bodily organs-in the sensitive appetites and wills of the flesh." (Romans7: 23, Amplified).

Paul found that this war going on with his flesh was winning because he would do what he didn't want to do and what he wanted to do, he couldn't (See Romans 7:19).

So how does one take off this old man in order to put on a new man; to not do what the flesh wants to do with its own lust and appetites? The Spirit is the one who can crucify your flesh, if you ask Him. "For if you live according to the flesh you will die: but, if by the Spirit you put to death the deeds of the body, you will live." (Romans 8:13, NKJV).

BEING PROACTIVE

Remember what works when breaking a stronghold. It needs to be repeated to walk daily in victory. You have three enemies to fight the world, the flesh and the devil.

"But thanks be to God, who gives us the victory through our Lord Jesus Christ." (1Corinthians 15:57, NKJV).

As we have already said, every morning be on guard; implement the **Prayer Strategy** as you start the day:
"This is the day the Lord hath made let us rejoice and be glad in it." (Psalm118: 24, NKJV)(start the day positive). Apply what you have learned.
Line up your flesh, and spirit man under the authority of the Holy Spirit.
"I say to my flesh be in submission to my spirit man."
"I say to my spirit man be in submission to the Holy Spirit."
"I now ask the Holy Spirit, to crucify my flesh and render it dead."

If the flesh is alive and not checked it will override your mind. The flesh will make every part of you its prisoner if you don't ask the Holy Spirit to help you put him to death. You cannot reform your old man-you must replace him with your new man.

You may not believe by declaring the above tactical prayers that it will work to break lust, anger, bitterness, and powerful desires of the flesh but it will. I've seen many people do it. Remember your words are powerful. It was by your words that you asked and received forgiveness for your sins from God. Your words can speak life and death they are so powerful. God spoke the worlds into existence with His words. We are made in His image.

Repeat those declarations at the beginning of every day; and your spirit man who knows what is right will begin to win over the flesh with the help of the Holy Spirit. The Holy Spirit is the agent in the book of Romans chapter eight, who can crucify the flesh so you may do what is right. "For if you live according to the flesh you will die (spiritually): but if by the Spirit you put to death the deeds of the body, you will live." (Romans 8:13, NKJV). I've seen many a person break hard addictions by doing this prayer strategy daily and finally they start winning the battle they've been fighting for all their lives.

"...The truly happy people are those who carefully study God's perfect law that makes people free, and they continue to study it. They do not forget what they have heard, but they obey what God's teaching says. Those who do this will be made happy."
(James 1:25, NCV).

Oswald Chambers said "Obedience to the Holy Spirit will mean that we have the power to direct our ideas, It is astonishing how we sit down under the dominance of an idea, whether a right or wrong idea, and the saints have sat down under this idea more than any other—that they cannot help thoughts of evil. Thank God that's a lie; we can."

Remember we learned a lie is as powerful as the truth if the person believes it. It will block their believing the opposite, which is the truth. It's one reason people stay in bondage. "...the Lord says: 'When people fall down, don't they get up again? When they discover they're on the wrong road, don't they turn back?

Then why do these people stay on their self-destructive path? Why do the people of Jerusalem refuse to turn back? They cling tightly to their lies and will not turn around. I listen to their conversations and don't hear a word of truth."(Jeremiah 8:4-6, NLT).

Time to give up the lie that you can't break it. You believe the lie because you've never been able to break it in the past. BUT DON'T BELIEVE THE LIE!

"For by the death He died, He died to sin [ending His relation to it] once for all, and the life, that He lives He is living to God-in unbroken fellowship with Him." (Romans 6:10, Amplified). Christ has won the victory for us –it's time we claimed it!

Jesus came to fulfill the prophecy in Isaiah 61:2 "...to proclaim liberty to the captives and open the prison to those who are bound." In Luke 4:18 He says He came to recover sight for the blind. The word used in the Greek is 'Typhlos" whose root word is 'Typhoo' meaning blind with pride. Don't let your pride keep you from seeing the truth. Admit you need God to enable you to overcome and He will do it. Let Christ's mind be in you in unbroken fellowship so you can think the way He does. Retrain your mind to listen to what you say to yourself. Watch what you are thinking it is imperative to know so you may control what you think.

AFTERCARE

Read the Word daily. Bring every thought captive, reading your **dashboard** and determine *does it line up with the Word?*

Seek the Mind of Christ to replace your old way of thinking.

Remember who you are in Christ, not what you or others have said you are.

Pray and journal what you feel God is saying to you.

John Eldredge in the 'Journey of Desire' writes: "We are at war, and the bloody battle is over our hearts. I am astounded how few Christians see this, how little they protect their hearts. We act as though we live in a sleepy little town during peacetime. We don't. We live in the spiritual equivalent of [a war-torn country]. Act like it, Watch over your heart. Don't let just anything in; don't let it go just anywhere. What's this going to do to my heart? It is a question that I ask in every situation.

What would happen if we prayed every day, 'O Lord God, help me measure my days and ask of everything I confront: What will this do to my heart?"

USE THE THREE LEGGED STOOL

The stool consists of three legs: a place, a time, and a method. If one leg of the stool is missing then the stool caves in. When someone tells me their devotional life is suffering I know one of these legs is missing (the set time, place, or method).

FIND A **PLACE** TO PRAY DAILY AND ALWAYS GO THERE.
ESTABLISH A **TIME** DAILY TO GO
TO THAT PLACE TO PRAY.
HAVE A **METHOD** THAT IS KNOW WHAT YOU
WILL DO WHEN YOU GO TO THAT PLACE.
(READ THE WORD, PRAY, JOURNAL ETC.).

Prayer helps us protect our hearts and minds by living in relationship with the Lord and staying under his protection. What comes in the mind affects our hearts that is our spirit man and will. Remember we are at war with these enemies: the world, the flesh, and the devil. He will help us win each battle as we depend on the Lord for our protection.

The **Word of God** is the sword of the Spirit the offensive weapon that is extremely powerful. Many a person has found if they just declare it out loud while refuting lies that are flooding their mind they can find the victory and the peace they desire.

"For the word of God is living and powerful, and sharper than any two-edged sword, piercing even to the division of soul and spirit, and of joints and marrow, and is a discerner of the thoughts and intents of the heart." (Hebrews 4:12-13, NKJV). The Word is essential to help one discern what is truth and what is not!

That is a very important reason why one should be in the Word daily.

Daily the war rages within us between the Spirit and the flesh the old man and the new man. It's the Holy Spirit that wins these battles for us whose job is to transform us to be like Christ. Start confessing your victory through the power of the Holy Spirit.

REMEMBER HOW POWERFUL YOUR WORDS ARE!

Mark Batterson shares, "In 1963, hall of fame pitcher Gaylord Perry made an offhanded comment before stepping into the batter's box: "They'll put a man on the moon before I hit a home run." That statement wasn't totally baseless, given the fact that most pitchers aren't great hitters. But it's rather ironic that Gaylord Perry hit his first and only home run of his baseball career six years later after Neil Armstrong set foot on the moon!

For better or for worse, our words double as self-fulfilling prophecies. Negative prophecies are validated by fear. Positive prophecies are validated by faith."

Part of learning something new requires unlearning what I used to believe. Professing in my words a new truth and renouncing the old belief.

Only when you remove a false belief is there even room to replace it with a true one. The old belief will stand in the way. Until I replace the notion it's unsafe to fly; and replace it with it's safer to fly than travel in a car. Then I'm not getting on the plane. I'm held back and restricted in my ability to travel very far. Unlearning is a big part of Learning.

~Don't let your words be negative, let them be positive spoken in prayer mixed with faith. Take a step toward the moon sitting with God in heavenly spiritually places, resting in His power to save always learning. ~

SUMMARY

We are created to live free!
What then should we remember to do?

Read and meditate on the scriptures found on the next page to discover and claim your true identity in Christ. This is very powerful to know who you really are in Christ.

Every day wake up and make these declarations preferably out loud:

Declare this is the day the Lord hath made; let us rejoice and enjoy it.

<u>Use the Prayer Strategy with Daily Declarations:</u>
I say to my flesh be in submission to my spirit man.
I say to my spirit man to be in submission to the Holy Spirit.
I ask the Holy Spirit to crucify my flesh.
I put on the whole armor of God: the helmet of salvation, the breastplate of righteousness, the belt of truth, the shoes of peace, the shield of faith, the sword of the Spirit and to pray always.

Keep the three-legged stool: determine a daily place, time, and method to pray and read the Word. Keep this daily appointment with God. You need it.

DON'T LET WHAT IS WRONG WITH YOU DEFINE YOU REMEMBER WHO YOU REALLY ARE IN CHRIST.

OUR REAL IDENTITY ACCORDING TO THE BIBLE

Scripture to read and meditate on
A Powerful exercise

Freedom in Christ ministries made up a scriptural guide to meditate on that tells us who we really are in Christ not whom we or ourselves tells us we are. When people meditate on who they really are according to the word they are set free from the lies that have held them.

I am accepted... John 1:12 I am God's child. John 15:15 As a disciple, I am a friend of Jesus Christ. Romans I have been justified.1 Corinthians 6:17 I am united with the Lord, and I am one with Him in spirit.1 Corinthians 6:19-20 I have been bought with a price and I belong to God.1 Corinthians 12:27 I am a member of Christ's body. Ephesians I have been chosen by God and adopted as His child. Colossians I have been redeemed and forgiven of all my sins. Colossians I am complete in Christ. Hebrews I have direct access to the throne of grace through Jesus Christ.

I am secure... Romans 8:1-2 I am free from condemnation. Romans I am assured that God works for my good in all circumstances. Romans I am free from any condemnation brought against me and I cannot be separated from the love of God.2 Corinthians 1:21-22 I have been established anointed and sealed by God. Colossians I am hidden with Christ in God. Philippians I am confident that God will complete the good work He started in me. Philippians I am a citizen of heaven.2 Timothy 1:7 I have not been given a spirit of fear but of power, love and a sound mind.1 John 5:18 I am born of God and the evil one cannot touch me.

I am significant... John 15:5 I am a branch of Jesus Christ, the true vine, and a channel of His life. John 15:16 I have been chosen and appointed to bear fruit. 1 Corinthians 3:16 I am God's temple. 2 Corinthians 5:17-21 I am a minister of reconciliation for God.

Ephesians 2:6 I am seated with Jesus Christ in the heavenly realm. Ephesians 2:10 I am God's workmanship. Ephesians 3:12 I may approach God with freedom and confidence. Philippians 4:13 I can do all things through Christ, who strengthens me. FREEDOM IN CHRIST MINISTRIES /WEB LOG/WWW.FICM.ORG

7

WHAT DOES A HEALED MIND LOOK LIKE THAT IS BASED ON CHRIST?

*Permit this mind to be in me that is in Christ Jesus.
If we can think like Christ then we can live
like him and that is His desire for us.*

The mind everyone wants is not fearful, not worried, but has entered God's rest walking in a supernatural peace. A mind that dwells in a state of contentment.

Actions of a healthy spiritual mind are:
- Let the peace of Christ rule in your heart. We are called to have peace. (see Colossians.3:15) " ...and God's peace [be yours, that tranquil state]...."guard over your hearts and minds in Christ Jesus." (Philippians 4:7,Amplified) We know from what we have learned that the God of peace

can crush satan under our feet from scripture in Romans 16:20.
- "Do not fret or have any anxiety about anything," (Philippians 4:6, Amplified).
- "...In everything by prayer... continue to make your wants known to God." (Philippians 4: 6, Amplified).
- I claim a healthy mind before God. I claim a mind at rest, calm, quiet, serene, a peaceful but alert mind. I claim this mind of Christ.
- Final outcome "...for I have learned in whatever state I am, to be content." (Philippians 4:11, NKJV). A person's soul excels when their heart is full of gratitude.

Pathway to achieve a new-contented mind:

- One must learn to be content, to be in peace, not fretting or worrying or anxious about anything. This supernatural peace will actually keep one content by guarding your heart and your mind -the way you think changes (See Romans 12: 2).

- One's mind is changed voluntarily and intentionally to become a different person by changing the way one thinks by following God's will. The word "repent" in the Greek is " metanoeo" meaning to have another mind or to change the mind.

- It's important to be patient in trouble and constantly praying. (see Romans 12:12).

- Studying the word (see 2 Timothy 2:15). Choosing to think the truth. (See Philippians 4: 8).

"Practice what you have learned and received and heard and seen in me, and model your way of living on it, and the God of peace—of untroubled, undisturbed well-being—will be with you."(Philippians 4: 9, Amplified).

To do this, one must have built a Godly stronghold or citadel around one's thoughts. As mentioned in 2 Corinthians 10:4-5 it teaches us to be "... casting down arguments and every high thing that exalts itself against the Knowledge of God, bringing every thought into captivity to the obedience of Christ."

You must decide to build a citadel around your mind to prevent any thoughts that are contrary to the way God thinks. You know this by your study of the Word of God and the Holy Spirit who guides you into all truth. Your mind must be saved from its old way of thinking and think the way Christ thinks. This is possible or God would not have offered it. To be of the same mind or "phoneo" means to direct one's mind to be the same. As we direct our thoughts to think more like Jesus through the Word and Prayer we begin to think the same as Jesus. We begin to have similar ways of thinking in the mind that grants us a much higher spiritual life and be freer to enjoy the life the creator always planned for us.

All this is possible as opposed to the thoughts and actions that separated you from God. "This includes you who were once far away from God. You were His enemies, separated from him by your evil thoughts and actions."(Colossians 1:21, NLT)

Remember Jesus prayer to the Father "...that they may be one, [just] as You, Father, are in Me, and I in you, that they may be one in Us..." (John17: 21-23,Amplified). This is a phenomenal request of the Father by the Son that we could be one in the Trinity and even learn to think the same. This will require spending time with God to learn His ways of thinking. Studying the Word of God is crucial. Having ongoing conversational prayer talking and learning new thoughts will help us claim this new mind. When that starts to occur as a person we start to bear supernatural fruit of the Spirit, new knowledge, anointing and power to work in the kingdom we didn't have before. It's a mind that becomes more and more free of blocks, distractions,, and enjoys the growth in knowledge and understanding. It's operating in the wisdom of the Most High that he said we could ask for liberally.

Pat Robertson says in his book "The Secret Kingdom". "I have become convinced that wisdom is the key to the secrets of the kingdom of God. It leads to favor. But the starting point is humility, as Solomon knew. For humility reveals the fear of, or reverence for the Lord.

The book of Proverbs reveals the next step: "the fear of the Lord is the beginning of wisdom, and knowledge of the Holy One is understanding. "(Proverbs 9:10, NIV).

The cycle is complete: from humility, to fear of the Lord, to wisdom, to knowledge of the Holy One.

Wisdom, or spiritual understanding, is knowledge of the Holy One. And that is what we are seeking-knowledge of God, knowledge of His will and purpose, knowledge of the invisible world and how it works, knowledge of how to reach into it and bring its blessing and prosperity into our visible world."

Through humbling ourselves and seeking the mind of Christ we gain knowledge only He has. That wisdom and understanding brings a richer and more abundant life we can't have any other way. We have to begin to change our thinking and replace it with God's.

"God is against the proud, but he gives grace to the humble. "(James 4: 6, NCV)

To establish ones identity in Christ we need to know it will never be instantaneous but changing over time. Renewing or reprograming our mind is a lifelong process.

Joyce Myers once said, on a tape I heard, that no one in the church ever told her she could control the way she thinks but she said she learned she could. And, so have I, and so can you. If you don't believe that then you will have to be stuck in obsessive thoughts and locked up by your enemy. The spider will control your mind instead of you. When we start controlling the way we think, and acting on what we see on the dashboard then we can start the great adventure of a new freedom.

Francois Fenelon said, "Happy is the soul that commits itself into the hands of it's Creator, ready to do His will, and continually cries 'Lord what will thou have me to do? Teach me to do your will, for you are my God." A soul is only happy when it's following the pathway the Creator has laid out for it.

Pursue a No-Spider Zone

We must learn to maintain a constant spirit of prayer that keeps us united with God. Then fight off anything in the world that tries to force us to give it up. Manage our thought life.

We were never created to live apart from the one who created us. In other words, we were not designed to ever be self-sufficient! Therefore, our soul, without this connection to God, will always be vulnerable to the spider and his webs of lies bringing us into bondage.

When you apply what you have learned in this book. Apply it's scriptures and truths as a remedy to break the spider's webs then use God's power to remove the spider who spun them, then you can be free to grow. Grow what? New fruit in your life that is absolutely awesome! Love, joy, peace, long suffering, kindness, goodness, faithfulness, gentleness, and self-control.

Thomas Kelly describes this life centered on God and what we can get. "LIFE FROM THE CENTER IS A LIFE OF UNHURRIED PEACE AND POWER, IT IS SIMPLE, SERENE, IT'S AMAZING. IT'S TRIUMPHANT, IT IS RADIANT IT TAKES NO TIME BUT OCCUPYS ALL OUR TIME AND IT MAKES OUR LIFE PROGRAM NEW AND OVERCOMING, WE NEED NOT GET FRANTIC- GOD IS AT THE HELM AND WHEN OUR LITTLE DAY IS DONE WE LIE DOWN IN PEACE FOR ALL IS WELL."

Do you long for a life like that? Then this book and the Bible declare, it is possible for you!

It may be that to dwell in the secret place of the Most High may not be in heaven. The secret place of the Most High may be referring to us, His temple. We are the ones to create an atmosphere for the Holy Spirit to move unimpeded within us. The more we control our thoughts and yield them to God, the better He can operate in us bearing His fruit.

Oswald Chambers said "It's possible to have a saved and sanctified experience and a stagnant mind. Learn how to make your mind awake and freer, when once your mind is awake never let it go to sleep. The brain does not need rest; it only needs a change of work. The intellect works with the greatest intensity when it works continuously; the more you do, the more you can do. We must work hard to keep in trim for God."

The best way of thinking is living the life God intended, a life whereby God becomes the center. Thomas Kelly shares more about a life from the center. "The practice of continuous prayer in the presence of God involves developing the habit of carrying on the mental life on two levels. At one level we are immersed in this world of time, but at a deeper level of our minds, we are in active relation with the Eternal life. Such practice of inward orientation...is the heart of religion." By 'heart of religion' he means at the core of our faith is a love relationship with God.

Steps in obedience with Christ as the center (Thomas Kelly thoughts in summary)
1.) Contemplate Jesus, Holy Spirit, through thoughts and Word.
2.) Obey His voice. Live in the present moment in submission and openness to Him.
3.) If you slip and stumble, get over it and restart again.

4.) Cease striving, submit to God, learn to live in His passive voice and let His life be willed through you.

You will have some experiences that may take you back, but learn from them and keep going.

Mark Batterson relates "During one of my nursing-home sermons, an octogenarian suffering from dementia stood up in the middle of my message and started undressing while yelling at the top of her lungs, "Get him out of here! Get him out of here!" Not much fazes you after that."

You can live through a situation, forgive, possibly laugh and move on. Your self-esteem comes from God not people.

Whoever dwells in the shelter of the Most High will rest in the shadow of the Almighty." (Psalm 91:1, NIV).

A practicing Christian must above all be one who practices the perpetual return of the soul into the sanctuary. Our inner sanctuary is a place we have prepared through repentance and love for God to dwell unimpeded with our will yielded to His. He will show us our defects constantly perfecting and cleansing within where He also dwells. We respond with a submissive and grateful heart that comes under His control. We become a temple that is His dwelling place. None of this will work without an active prayer relationship with the Lord. In fact it is best to cultivate a prayer life that becomes as natural as breathing. Without this kind of breathing one slowly dies spiritually.

"The secret places of the heart cease to be our noisy workshop.

They become a holy sanctuary of adoration and self-oblation, where we are kept in perfect peace, if our minds be stayed on Him who has found us in the inward springs of our life." (Thomas Kelly)

"Come to Me, all you who labor and are heavy laden, and I will give you rest." (Matthew11: 28,NIV). God bids His people to come to Him, as He will help them, reassure them, and give them rest. Jesus said that He is the way, the truth, and the life, our hope and salvation. In other words, when you come to Him, He can promise rest from any problem because He can always provide a way through every problem. He can give you hope and salvation for every problem. He promised there would always be a way of escape from every spider web through Him; you only need to come to Him.

A GOOD DAILY HABIT TO COME TO HIM

"He who dwells in the secret place of the Most High
shall abide under the shadow of the Almighty.
I will say of the Lord, "He is my refuge and my fortress;
My God, in Him I will trust."(Psalm 91:1-2, NKJV).

It is in this secret place that your life is led by the Spirit and therefore excels. On one level you live in the world; but it is here you live on a much deeper level with God. This sanctuary as one grows closer to God becomes more and more holy –that is less of the person and more of God taking up residence. The dysfunctional soul is the one who is disconnected from his creator. Therefore nothing new can be created. The source of possible healing is cut off. "For whoever wants to save his life, will lose it, but whoever loses his life because of Me will find it." (Matt.16: 25, HCSB).

The privilege of actually becoming one with the Most High God is given up.
The more we die to self the more we become one with God and desire to be with him even more. One purpose of talking and being with God is learning to be like Him. If we lose our life we will find it in our identity with Christ. We will discover in prayer and the Word who we really are and how we were created to function.

When we were full of ourselves in the world —we discovered we were too empty of God. The Spirit invokes in us a need to have more of God in us.

This is a lifelong pursuit into eternity always becoming what the Creator created us to be that is discovered as we become more one with God in our inner spirit man.

"Two main points of attention are necessary to maintain a constant spirit of prayer that unites us with God. We must continually seek to cherish it, and we must avoid anything that tends to make us lose it. In order to cherish it, we should follow a regular course of reading; we must have appointed times of secret prayer and frequently recall our minds consciously to God during the day." (Francois Fenelon)

> "We have to lose our way of thinking and form Jesus Christ's way. Acquire your soul with patience." It takes time and discipline. When we are regenerated and have the life of the Son of God in us." (Oswald Chambers).

Like great spiritual leaders from the past we become regenerated or transformed the same way they did by the reprogramming of our minds to Christ's through the word and prayer. What a privilege this is and a most unexpected gift! The more we become dependent on Christ the more independent we become on the world. "You're a soul made by God, made for God, which means you were not made to be self-sufficient." (Dallas Willard) It's important to remember it's all doable. We only have to claim what is ours. We just do it in God's strength and not our own. In fact He has already done it,

"For He has rescued us from the kingdom of darkness and transferred us into the Kingdom of His dear Son, who purchased our freedom and forgave our sins." (Colossians 1:13-14, NLT).

"The most remarkable thing about the mastership of Jesus Christ is that He never insists on being Master. We often feel that if only He would insist, we would obey Him. Obedience to Jesus Christ is essential, but never compulsory; He will never take means to make me obey Him. Jesus Christ will always make up for my deficiencies; He always forgives my disobedience, but if I am going to be a disciple, it is essential for me to obey Him." (Oswald Chambers).

"For we are God's Masterpiece. He has created us anew in Christ Jesus, so we can do good things He planned for us long ago." (Ephesians 2:10, NLT). Did you hear the Master is making a masterpiece out of us?

"The brain is a wonderful organ; it starts working the moment you get up in the morning and does not stop until you get into the office." Robert Frost

Use your brain all the time in conjunction with the mind of Christ.

The brain was created magnificent by God. We only need Him to help us use it properly the way He created it.

~ **"God began doing a good work in you, and I am sure he will continue it until it is finished when Jesus comes again." (Philippians 1: 6, NCB).** ~

Scripture
To encourage you on your journey

"Be strong and of good courage, do not fear nor be afraid of them; for the lord your God, he is the one who goes with you. He will not leave you nor forsake you."(Deuteronomy 31:6, NKJV).

"The Lord is near. Do not be anxious about anything, but in every situation, by prayer and petition, with thanksgiving, present your requests to God. And the peace of God, which transcends all understanding, will guard your hearts and your minds in Christ Jesus." (Philippians 4: 5-7, NIV).

"I have learned the secret of being content in any and every situation, whether well fed or hungry, whether living in plenty or in want. I can do all this through him who gives me strength." (Philippians 4: 12-13, NIV).

"...if God be for us, no one can defeat us? " (Romans 8:31, NCV).

"He gives strength to those who are tired and more power to those who are weak. " (Isaiah 40:29, NCV) "but the people who trust the Lord will become strong again." (Isaiah 40: 31, NCV).

"God is our protection and our strength. He always helps in times of trouble." (Psalm 46:1, NCV).

"We also have joy with our troubles, because we know that these troubles produce patience. And patience produces character, and character produces hope. And this hope will never disappoint us, because God has poured out his love to fill our hearts." (Romans 5:3-5, NCV)."

Final Conclusion

If like others you have attempted to try any of the above Godly remedies, then I know you have found some encouragement if not victory. The reason is because God has ordained it.

Jesus said it was for this reason that He came. Jesus, in Luke 4, quoted a scripture from Isaiah 61 that he said He came to fulfill.

"The Spirit of the Lord GOD is upon me, Because the LORD has anointed Me To preach good tidings to the poor; He has sent Me to heal the brokenhearted, To proclaim liberty to the captives, And the opening of the prison to those who are bound; To proclaim the acceptable year of the LORD, And the day of vengeance of our God; To comfort all who mourn, To console those who mourn in Zion (The Church), to give them beauty for ashes, the oil of joy for mourning..." (Isaiah 61:1-3, NKJV)

May I encourage you, don't make this hard just do it. Jesus already won the battle. No matter how big the stronghold, it's God's power that wins the fight not yours. You only have to act doing the simple prayers mentioned with meaning in your heart. He will come through in your weakness, which is how His strength is actually perfected or completed.

All who believe and apply the Word with God's help can find salvation from their sins, and their mind that is holding them captive, and healing for their broken hearted emotions. Also they may receive physical healing as it says in His Word.

> "My son, attend to my words; incline
> thine ear unto my sayings.
> Let them not depart from thine heart.
> For they are life unto those that find them,
> and health to all flesh." (Proverbs 4:20-22, KJV)

The words shared are for those who discover it's power, and believe they bring healing. "If you will listen carefully to the voice of the Lord your God and do what is right in His sight, obeying His commands and keeping all His decrees, then I will not make you suffer any of these diseases I sent on the Egyptians (the world); for I am the Lord who heals you." (Exodus 15: 26, NLT).

If you will listen and believe, then ask God to heal your body as he has promised, as well as your spirit, emotions and mind.

Important Things to Remember
THE TAKE AWAYS:

*Use the <u>Dashboard</u> an awareness must be cultivated to start listening to your self-talk while watching the thoughts on your dashboard that come through your mind. This must become a regular habit! You can do this and it will get better with practice. Your dashboard will also tell you by what you feel that something needs your attention right away. I would feel dark ominous thoughts and would know immediately the spirit of fear was coming against me.

"Just as you drive a car and can read the dashboard so you can go through the day and read your thoughts."

When your see and recognize something is invading you not of God then immediately capture/isolate it and ask the

Holy Spirit to delete it. Do it as often as needed until you are free. God gave you the ability with His help to control what you choose to think or not think. Use this ability everyday the rest of your life.

"He would not ask you to bring every thought captive if you could not do it."

*You may have to exercise the prayers several times in a 5 minute period to begin with, then every hour, then daily. Months later you may need to capture the same thoughts, as the spider tries to come back into your mind and spin a web. But each time it gets easier to control those thoughts and keep your victory. The spider may return in times of stress; but maintain your victory by <u>watching the dashboard</u>.

REMEMBER FAILURE IS AN EVENT NOT A PERSON.

* If you fail, get over it, and return to what you have learned that works with the Holy Spirit's help. You are not wasting time but learning to overcome in Christ. The word says, to he who overcomes will he rule with me later in my kingdom. You are becoming stronger not weaker in your prayer life. You are growing and becoming much deeper in your relationship with the Lord.

* Use the <u>prayer strategy</u> mentioned in order to build a stronghold of your own around your mind and spirit man. Daily line up your flesh under your spirit man and your spirit man under the Holy Spirit. Pray each piece of the spiritual armor on you. These prayers take less than 5 minutes -I do it every morning. There may be other ways to accomplish one's needed victory in the Lord, but I know all that has been shared works from my personal experience and working with so many others.

*The most critical decision is to decide you want the victory over the spider and the web that is holding you. Then with that determination apply what you have learned above and with the power of Almighty God you will win and live free at last. Think about what God can do and not what you haven't been able to do up till now. Do not be defined by the past but what you will be in Christ.

*If you have faith to believe He has taken away your sins then you have the same faith needed to believe he will take away all your diseases.

> "Bless the Lord, O my soul,
> And forget not all His benefits:
> Who forgives all your iniquities
> Who heals all your diseases
> Who redeems your life from destruction..."
> (Psalm103: 2-3, NKJV).

~ DON'T FORGET ALL THESE BENEFITS THAT ARE YOURS! USE THEM FOR YOUR CONTINUAL TRANSFORMATION. ~

NOTES AND REFERENCES
In order of how they appear in this book.

All Oswald Chambers quotes are taken form: "The Quotable Oswald Chambers" compiled & edited by David McCasland, 2008 Discovery House Publisher appearing as used in this book found on P.244, P.97, P.90, P.151, P.80, P.163, P.164, and P.176.

Billy Graham story with little boy: www.jollynotes.com, P.4.

(The World Fears,) "In a Pit on a Snowy Day with a Lion" Mark Batterson, 2006 Multnomah, P.47

Bandit of Joy, "Applause of Heaven " by Max Lucado, 1990 Word Publishing P.77-86.

Martin Luther King "forgiveness" quote. www. goodreads.com 1-9-1

Robert Muller "forgiveness" quote. www.goodreads.com 1-9-14

Nelson Mandela "forgiveness" quote. www.goodreads.com 1-9-14

"God's Promises for You", Max Lucado, 2005 Countryman division of Thomas Nelson P.83

Albert Einstein, quote Mark Batterson "The Grave Robber" Baker Books, 2014 ,P.127

Henry Cloud, Quote www.goodreads com,P.1-30.

Dear Jesus story "www.jollynotes.com P.39

Ben Bailey joke " www.thoughtcatalog.Com, P.42

John Eldredge quote "The Jeremiah Study Bible, Worthy Publishing, 2013 Page767

"The Bullet proof George Washington" by David Barton Aledo, TX:Wallbuilder Press.

Gaylord Perry story. Mark Batterson "The Grave Robber" 2014 Baker Books P.120

Freedom in Christ Ministries/web log/www.FICM.org

Neil Anderson, "The Bondage Breaker "Quote from "Praying God's Word". Beth Moore 2000 B & H Publishing Group P.29

Francis Frangipane, "Holiness, Truth, and the Power of God" quote from "Praying God's Word" Beth Moore 2000 B & H publishing Group 2000 P.181

Tullian Tchividjian, "Jesus +Nothing= Everything," www.goodreads.com 1-30-62

Brennan Manning, "The Ragamuffin Gospel" Multnomah publishers, Inc. 1990 P.192

Pat Robertson, "The Secret Kingdom", 1982 Thomas Nelson Publishers P.93-94

Francois Fenelon, "Talking with God" 1997 Paraclete Press P.130

Thomas Kelly, Christian Mystics.com/traditional Quakers

Mark Batterson, "Wild Goose Chase" 2008 Multnomah books P.35.

Francois Fenelon "Talking With God" 1997 Paraclete Press P.7.

Dallas Willard, "Soul Caring" by John Ortberg, 2014 Zondervan P.39

Robert Frost, www.Braineyquote.com, K2BX 99

A Good Prayer, John Ballie, 1949 John Scribner's Sons P.131

All Scripture translations are indicated when quoted. Those used are:
"New International Bible" NIV@1972, 1978,1984,2011.
"The New Living Translation"
"The Amplified Bible"
"The Message Bible"
"New King James Version"
"King James Version"

About The Author

Phil Bennett is a prayer strategist with a BA degree in psychology and a master of arts degree in biblical studies. He has been used to mobilize many thousands of hours of continuous prayer across America, the United Kingdom, Africa, France, Germany, Latin America and Asia. While serving in pastoral ministry in North Carolina, Phil travels the world to spread the vision that God answers prayer. He has been used in the local church to minister spiritual healing to believer's. Phil has been called to engage in spiritual warfare on behalf of both individual people and nations.

Other books are "SAMUEL a Spiritual Life Lived To The Highest", "A SINGLE WEAPON Formed Against The Enemy That Will Prosper", "WATCHMEN OF THE LORD"with well known author Dick Eastman.

55453866R00070

Made in the USA
Charleston, SC
28 April 2016